SMART PACKING

for Today's Traveler

by Susan Foster

Edited by Barbara Weiland
Designed by Linda Wisner

Third Edition

SMART
TRAVEL
PRESS

PORTLAND
OREGON

For my mother and late father, Hazel and Bill John. Thank you for the gift of the love of travel. Even though you grew up during the Depression, your thrifty nature did not stifle your travel gene. We experienced the joy of new places on a slim budget, but we traveled.

And, for my dear husband, David Bosworth. This book could never have become a reality without your loving support. Thanks for being my cheerleader and my best friend.

Publisher's Cataloging-In-Publication Data
(Prepared by The Donohue Group, Inc.)

Foster, Susan (Susan Pletsch)
    Smart packing for today's traveler / by Susan Foster ; edited by Barbara Weiland ; designed by Linda Wisner ; illustrations by Jeannette Schilling, Kate Pryka, and Diane Russell. -- 3rd ed.

    p. : ill. ; cm.

    Includes bibliographical references and index.
    ISBN: 978-0-9702196-7-1

1. Travel--Handbooks, manuals, etc. 2. Luggage--Packing--Handbooks, manuals, etc. I. Weiland, Barbara. II. Wisner, Linda. III. Schilling, Jeannette. IV. Pryka, Kate. V. Russell, Diane, 1949- VI. Title.

G151 .F67 2008
910/.2/02   2008900628

Published by Smart Travel Press
Portland, OR
www.smartpacking.com

Design and Production by Wisner Creative, Portland, Oregon
Illustrations by Jeannette Schilling, Kate Pryka, and Diane Russell

Printed in USA
on recycled paper

"Wrinkled suits, overstuffed luggage, fo
liquids. At some point, every traveler has suffered the consequences
of poor packing. Susan Foster, author of SMART PACKING FOR TODAY'S
TRAVELER shares her best tips to pack like a pro."
Margaret Loftus, National Geographic Traveler

"The book covers every cranny of packing: outfit planning, luggage
picking, type of trip (adventure or business, kids or cruise)."
Andrea Sachs, The Washington Post

"This book is filled with tips, anecdotes and recommendations...
her Web site, www.smartpacking.com, offers updates..."
Tod Jones, The Costco Connection

"How to be the leader of the pack for your next trip? Follow Susan
Foster's five easy steps: Plan. Select. Edit. Pack. Go."
Sylvi Capelaci, Toronto Sun

"As airlines continue to limit the number, size and weight of bags that
can be checked or carried on, packing lighter and smarter is more
important than ever....Susan Foster, author of SMART PACKING, offers
a number of tips that can be applied to the business traveler or family
taking their dream vacation." *Associated Press*

"She also addresses ways to maintain creature comforts and good
health while traveling, and offers valuable insight into a bevy of helpful
travel gadgets. This paperback is the most thorough book I've found
on the subject." Colleen Birch Maile, SkyWest Magazine

"There are hundreds of tips in this thoroughly illustrated book."
The Desert Sun, Palm Springs, CA

"Foster's book offers plenty of advice, but the tip I like best is the
amount of clothing you take should not be in direct proportion to the
length of your vacation or business trip."
The Sun, San Bernardino, CA

"SMART PACKING is absolutely the last word on the subject of packing...There are lots and lots of line drawings of all kinds of clothing,
luggage, baby transport, accessories, men's wear and women's, carry-on
baggage tags, etc." *Travelwriter Marketletter*

"Smart packing all comes down to planning—and what to do with your
underwear.... SMART PACKING includes tips and gadget suggestions to
make the journey easier and more enjoyable." *Melissa Worden,
USAToday.com*

"...While most people feel a two-week trip requires major changes of
clothing, you'll be better off packing cleverly instead of in quantity.
Consult a book such as SMART PACKING FOR TODAY'S TRAVELER."
Donald D. Groff, Newark Star-Ledger, Newark, NJ

"Packing light is easier said than done. SMART PACKING offers tips on how and what to pack in a small suitcase."
Kiplinger's Retirement Report

"Foster, well-traveled and author of SMART PACKING FOR TODAY'S TRAVELER, has many tips for packing well, starting with choosing the right suitcase and ending with a checklist for closing down your home....addresses situations from traveling with a baby to traveling on business." *Janet Filips, The Oregonian*

"There are step-by-step hints to help you follow the basic rules she outlines, as well as over 400 illustrations that make the book fun to read as well." *Eve Carr, www.bellaonline.com*

"Want to learn how to look smart and pack less? Susan Foster, author of SMART PACKING FOR TODAY'S TRAVELER, offers advice on her site, smartpacking.com." *Carol Pucci, The Seattle Times*

"Lots of 'how to pack' books have crossed our desks over the years, most pretty predictable. However, SMART PACKINGis in a class of its own; invest in a copy and you'll never need another packing book." *Ann Wallace, Travel Scoop*

"One of the best sources I have ever found for invaluable travel information." *Ada Duncan, "The Senior Times," The News-Review, Roseburg, OR*

"SMART PACKING FOR TODAY'S TRAVELER is a terrific book...turn to Foster for practical advice and failure-resistant methods on organizing your trip without bringing too much stuff, finding the best bag, and how to reduce and maintain when you have too much." *William Tomicki, syndicated column*

"An absolute MUST for successful packing!" *www.CruiseDiva.com*

"...Reveals all her travel secrets that take the rest of us a lifetime to learn by trial and error." *Barbara Christy Wagner, Senior Wire syndicate*

"Think you know how to pack? You don't. But globetrotter Susan Foster knows. Her illustrated guide covers everything you thought you knew but couldn't compartmentalize. Face it, if packing were just a matter of common sense, my underwear wouldn't hang out of my notebook case...SMART PACKING has something for everyone." *dingbatmag.com review*

"Heavy luggage can lighten your wallet...SMART PACKING FOR TODAY'S TRAVELER offers tips to avoid this." *Marshall Loeb, CBS MarketWatch (and syndicated)*

Table of Contents

About the Author

Susan (Pletsch) Foster has been traveling for over thirty years and has spent her entire career living out of a suitcase. Foster is the perfect person to give advice on travel clothes and packing; she has packed and unpacked over 5,000 times!

© OWEN CAREY

After graduating with a degree in Home Economics from Arizona State University, (Pletsch) Foster traveled as a teacher in the sewing industry. Eventually, she co-founded Palmer/ Pletsch Associates, a leading publisher of sewing books.

Susan Pletsch and Pati Palmer became household names in the sewing world by writing and promoting four books, publishing eight others, and designing sewing patterns for Vogue and later McCall's (where Palmer/Pletsch designs still appear). Pletsch and Palmer and a talented teaching staff criss-crossed the United States and Canada presenting sewing seminars and refining their travel and packing skills.

(Pletsch) Foster later sold her interest in her business and married a man involved in international trade. Her travels then took her on a global marathon as she accompanied her husband on business trips around the world. Foster watched American tourists arrive in Hong Kong with huge suitcases and was surprised to notice these people wearing the same outfits, day after day. She deduced that they had brought bags of clothing, but not the right things. If she could pack for three weeks in one bag and be well dressed for business meetings and dinners and comfortable on tourist expeditions, then she knew she had information and experience that would help others accomplish the same thing. Years of research amassing information led to the publication of *Smart Packing for Today's Traveler.*

Foster – now spokesperson and speaker – continues to share her packing expertise on radio shows, television and in person.

Read This First!

Study now, go later.

Are you one of those travelers who throws things in a suitcase one hour before leaving for the airport, all the while praying to the packing gods that you have the right things to wear on arrival? If so, this book is for you. Even if you think you plan carefully for every trip, you're sure to learn some great travel tips in the pages that follow. I can say that with confidence because during my professional career, I have packed and unpacked at least five thousand times. I know how to choose and pack travel clothing that works!

In *Smart Packing for Today's Traveler*, you'll learn how to select the right things to wear for your trip and how to pack efficiently so your trip is the important event, and what to pack for it is easy and automatic. As I wrote this book, I surveyed well-traveled friends and included their creative travel tips throughout.

Smart Packing for Today's Traveler is divided into four major parts. You may want and need to read it from cover to cover before your next trip. Or, you may have specific travel questions that require solutions before you pack your bags tomorrow. Either way, you'll find what you need in one of the following sections.

Part I: Plan Your Perfect Trip

Here you'll find everything you need to know to plan your trip so you can choose the right clothes and accessories, toiletries and cosmetics. You'll learn how to: pack light; plan for changing weather; choose clothing appropriate for anywhere in the world; and purchase new clothing made of travel-friendly fabrics. I've even included goof-proof packing lists.

Part II: Pack Smart

Looking for new luggage? Don't go shopping until you've read this section! You'll do a personal luggage profile and learn about current trends in luggage so you can choose wisely — whether you're starting fresh or adding to what you already own. You'll also learn how to pack as efficiently and wrinkle-free as possible; what to check and what to carry-on; and how to deal with delayed or lost baggage.

Part III: Customize Your Wardrobe

Where you're going and what you'll be doing have a dramatic effect on what to pack for your trip. Perhaps you're headed for an important business meeting halfway around the world, an African safari, a romantic cruise, or a family vacation with the kids. If so, check out the appropriate chapter for advice on how to plan and pack wisely for maximum comfort and fun along the way!

Part IV: Travel Safely in Comfort and Good Health

Packing wisely also means planning for contingencies and packing the things that are needed to make your trip as carefree as possible. In Part IV, you'll learn what to take along (besides clothes) and what to do for health and safety while you're away; how to plan for finances and insurance on the road; travel gadgets that are worth packing; what to wear for comfort en route; and how to take care of your clothing on extended trips.

Last, be sure to read "Going Home." It includes information about packing for the return trip, how to handle customs, and things to do at home that will ensure an even better next trip.

Every chapter contains personal anecdotes and tips including:

SMART TRAVEL *Tip*

Clever travel tidbits to make your trip easier or more enjoyable.

SMART TRAVEL *Gadget*

Unusual or particularly useful travel accessories.

SMART TRAVEL *Item*

Unique clothing or accessories that make travel easier, for example, pants that convert to shorts with clever zip-off legs (see page 40).

SMART TRAVEL *Security Update*

Important information for travelers about airport security regulations. For the most current rules, please go to www.smartpacking.com.

FIVE STEPS to Smart Packing

1. **PLAN** where and when you will travel and the length of the trip so that weather, culture, and special events can be considered.

2. **SELECT** the most appropriate and comfortable clothing, plus the best accessories and travel extras. Lay them out in an undisturbed area so you can edit or add as needed.

3. **EDIT** so everything fits into the best bag for your trip.

4. **PACK** all of the above using the most efficient packing techniques and tips.

5. **GO**. Travel lightly and under your own power to any destination and be comfortable, well dressed, and happy.

PLAN.

SELECT.

EDIT.

PACK.

GO.

It's that easy!

PART I:

PLAN YOUR PERFECT TRIP

The amount of clothing you take is not in proportion to the length of your trip!

Discover how to pack less and still have more to wear.

CHAPTER 1

Planning Makes Perfect

Planning ahead is best, but short-notice trips can be fun too! Study the chapters you need now so you can be ready to go anywhere, anytime.

Perfect trips don't just happen. Planning two to three months ahead lets you take advantage of advance reservation discounts, to guarantee space, and allows time to read up on the special features of your destination. Trip planning involves:

1. Deciding where you want to go and when, and how long you will be gone.

2. Creating an itinerary. Where will you be and what will you do on each morning, afternoon, and evening?

3. Making travel arrangements.

4. Planning what you will wear for each event on your itinerary and for the possibility of unexpected events.

A professional travel agent can help. Look for professional certi-fication and ask for recommendations from friends who are fre-quent travelers. A good travel agent can make the difference between a great trip and an awful one. A good travel agent can get the best fares, recommend the perfect hotel, suggest and book interesting activities, and pass on clothing tips. Travel agents are paid a commission by airlines, hotels, and car rental agencies. In some cases they may charge you an additional fee for services — ask first so there are no surprises.

Look for guidebooks at the library or local bookstore to learn all about your destination. Use the most recent edition — times, events, and prices do change. In addition, try these helpful travel information sources:

• Check travel and destination websites on the internet.

• Read your local newspaper travel section — an excellent and current resource.

• Buy or read at the library recent copies of national travel magazines such as *Conde Nast Traveler, Travel & Leisure,* and *National Geographic Traveler* (see "Resources," page 237).

- Ask your well-traveled friends and family members for their favorite places at your destination.
- Check websites, write or call local, state, or country tourism offices for valuable (usually free) information and maps.

Organize Your Itinerary

Use this four-step process to create an activity-based, visual picture of your trip so you always pack the right things to wear.

1. On a piece of paper, mark large calendar spaces for each day you will be away. Divide each day into "Morning," "Afternoon," and "Evening."

2. Note arrival and departure times in the appropriate spaces.

Itinerary Calendar

	S	M	T	W	Th
MORNING				**1** 8 a.m. depart blue pant suit cream tee-shirt (take yellow sweater in carry-on)	**2** yellow tee-shirt print pants blue jacket Brunch 11 a.m.
AFTERNOON				4 p.m. arrive	sightseeing
EVENING				dinner – casual	dinner – casual
MORNING	**5** 10 a.m. museums all day	**6** antique shopping	**7** khakis denim shirt yellow sweater	**8** blue pant suit white tee-shirt 11 a.m. depart	**9**
AFTERNOON	white tee-shirt print pants blue jacket	khakis red tee-shirt denim shirt	1 p.m. half-day tour		
EVENING	dinner 8 p.m. Le Club navy dress metallic shawl	dinner – casual	dinner 8 p.m. dancing! navy dress metallic shawl	6 p.m. arrive home	

Add planned activities: work appointments, sightseeing tours, lunch reservations at a special restaurant, for example.

3. List all the activities you want to participate in (from guidebooks and your research) and add them to your itinerary. Make advance reservations if possible.

4. Decide what will you wear for each of these activities on each day of the itinerary. As you fill in your calendar, don't choose a different outfit for each day away from home. The amount of clothing you take is not in proportion to the length of your trip! I take the same amount of clothing for one week as I do for three; my underwear just gets laundered more often.

F	S
3 *tour all day* *8 a.m.* *pick-up* *khakis* *white polo* *yellow* *sweater* *dinner* *- casual*	4 *shopping* *noon - lunch at* *Holly's* *navy dress* *yellow sweater* *shopping -* *eat at mall*
10	11

Determine Your Travel Style

The "style" of your trip will make a big difference in what you plan to wear. Are you planning a trip to a major city, a countryside tour of smaller towns, an exciting adventure tour, or a stay at a resort? Each of these requires a different style of clothing.

Your travel clothing should be comfortable and allow you to blend in with the local population as much as possible. (Be sure to read "Worldwide Wardrobing," beginning on page 36.) The term "travel style" relates to the tone of your destination, your planned activities, plus your personal fashion choice. On the next two pages I have identified four different travel styles that may be useful to consider as you plan your travel wardrobe for a particular trip.

Sophisticate

Visiting a major city requires more conservative, sophisticated, and dressier clothing than you might wear at home. This is especially important for business travel, but should also be considered for pleasure travel. Cities have a business clothing attitude for most events, plus there is more focus on fashion in cities. What will you do in the city? Stay at a casual motel or at a fashionable hotel where just sitting in the lobby demands dressing up? Will you dine at fine, elegant restaurants where a coat and tie are often required or will you eat at small, casual cafés?

Casual

A trip to the country calls for casual clothing, often with a conservative attitude. Fashion on the cutting edge is more at home in the city. Think about your activities and your accommodations. Will you be staying at a casual bed and breakfast or at a charming country inn that may require a coat and tie for dinner? Will you be joining friends for dinner at the local country club (oops, there's that coat and tie again) or is a casual, at-home barbecue in the plans?

Resort/Sport

Sports such as golf, tennis, and skiing have specific clothing requirements. It's the social attire for the resorts that can be confusing. Coat and tie is generally the exception while playful clothing is more common. Chic ski resorts in Europe are high-fashion and glitzy for dining; women wear fur coats with snow boots and carry their high-heeled dancing shoes. Don't try that in Sun Valley, Idaho, where clean jeans and cowboy boots can go just about anywhere. To determine the appropriate tone of dress, check with your travel agent or hotel.

Adventurer

To go where few others have gone often requires totally different clothing. You will need sturdy, comfortable, easy-care clothing for adventure travel. Several catalogs now feature a wide range of high-performance adventure clothing — the selection has never been better. Even though there are few dress codes in the back country, it's a good idea to pack more conservative attire. Higher neck-lines and longer shorts are less likely to offend the local population and will provide better sun and bug protection.

Consider the Weather

Before you can make any decisions about clothing for your trip, you need a very important piece of information — what will the weather be like at your destination? You'll want to know the average temperature and how much rain is likely at the time of your trip. A few degrees in temperature can mean you're comfortably dressed or miserable, and who wants to get caught in a downpour without an umbrella? Packing the right things can make the difference between a great trip and one that is less than fun!

How comfortable you will be depends on the local temperature, humidity, and wind. Rain and snow will also affect how you feel. Depending on the weather, you will need either a winter wardrobe or a summer one, but for some destinations or extended trips, both will be required. See page 35 for more about packing for two climates. Here are some weather facts you'll need to know to plan effectively:

- Is the summer heat dry or humid with frequent rain showers?
- Is air conditioning common in the area? Is there central heating in cold climates?
- Is it sunny and cold, or windy, rainy, and cold where you're headed?

How Hot is Hot?

Mary and Jerry live on the Oregon Coast where the highest temperature in the past year was 78°F. One summer they traveled to Turkey and, knowing it would be hot, they packed cotton shorts and tee-shirts. When they arrived, it was 90°F and humid. They were forced to shop for cooler clothing — their Oregon clothes were too heavy to be tolerable.

When gathering weather information for your destination, be sure to ask specifics: how hot is hot, how humid is humid? Ask your hosts, travel agent, friends who have been there **"What do you wear to be comfortable?"**

Luckily, Mary and Jerry were able to buy inexpensive, lighter weight items that fit. "An excuse to shop — what fun," you might say! Not if you are in Europe where clothing is very expensive; not if you are a medium-sized American trying to shop in Bangkok where clothing is sized for the tiny Thai people. Shopping as entertainment is one thing but shopping out of necessity is another. It is best to take the right things with you.

Check Your Destination Weather

To learn about the weather at your destination, you can:

- Check weather on-line at www.weather.com or http://weather.usatoday.com, or download weather from these sources to your desktop, PDA, or cell phone.

- Watch The Weather Channel on cable TV.

- Read your local newspaper or *USA Today*.

- Check your destination guidebook. Guides usually list monthly or seasonal average temperatures and rainfall and often suggest appropriate clothing.

Continue to monitor the weather until your departure. You can always toss in a pair of silk long underwear or substitute a lighter weight shirt if the weather changes at the last minute.

Convert Temperature Scales

The temperature scale used in the United States is Fahrenheit (shown as °F). Centigrade or Celsius (shown as °C) is the most widely used scale throughout the rest of the world.

To convert temperatures quoted in °C to °F, double the Centigrade figure and add 30.

$$20°C \times 2 = 40 + 30 = 70°F$$

To convert °F to °C, subtract 30 and divide by 2.

$$70°F - 30 = 40 \div 2 = 20°C$$

This works with temperatures above 0°C. Or, you can photocopy the chart below and take it with you.

CENTIGRADE

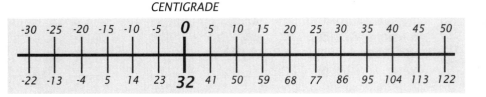

FAHRENHEIT

What About Wind Chill?

The wind can make hot temperatures feel cooler or make cold temperatures dangerously cold. Temperature and wind together create a "wind chill temperature" that is lower than the actual temperature reading. Cold plus wind can result in hypothermia and frostbite. To guard against both, it's best to layer warm and wicking clothing under a windproof outer shell. (See "Carefree Travel Fabrics" on page 74 for more on wicking fibers.) If you know the wind speed, then the Wind Chill Index can give you an idea of how to dress for comfort.

WIND MPH	TEMPERATURE							DANGER ZONE
	15°	10°	5°	0°	-5°	-10°	-15°	
	WINDCHILL FACTOR							
5	10	5	0	-5	-10	-15	-20	
10	0	-10	-15	-20	-25	-35	-45	
15	-10	-20	-25	-30	-40	-45	-50	
20	-15	-25	-30	-35	-45	-50	-60	

What About the Heat Index?

Heat plus humidity creates a higher real temperature, which means you will feel hotter. Find the temperature along the left side of the chart and the humidity along the top; where the two numbers intersect is the heat index. Some weather-reporting agencies now use this index as a summertime heads-up when hot weather can be dangerous to your health.

When the heat index is high, dress in lightweight, light-colored clothing; stay in the shade or air-conditioned places; and drink plenty of water. For specific clothing suggestions, see "Dressing for Hot Weather," beginning on page 30.

RELATIVE HUMIDITY (%)

AIR TEMPERATURE - FAHRENHEIT	40	45	50	55	60	65	70	75	80	85	90	95	100	
110	136													
108	130	137												
106	124	130	137											
104	119	124	131	137										
102	114	119	124	130	137									
100	109	114	118	124	129	136								
98	105	109	113	117	122	128	134							EXTREME DANGER
96	101	104	108	112	116	121	126	132						
94	97	100	103	106	110	114	119	124	129	136				
92	94	96	98	101	105	108	112	116	121	126	131			
90	91	93	95	97	100	103	106	109	113	117	122	127	132	DANGER
88	88	89	91	93	95	98	100	103	106	110	113	117	121	
86	85	87	88	89	91	93	95	97	100	102	105	108	112	
84	83	84	85	86	88	89	90	92	94	96	98	100	103	CAUTION
82	81	82	83	84	84	85	86	88	89	90	91	93	95	
80	80	80	81	81	82	82	82	84	84	86	86	86	87	

CHAPTER 2

Choosing the Right Clothes

Your travel wardrobe depends on the size of the suitcase and what you can manage without unnecessary stress.

Frequent travelers begin thinking about clothes one week before a routine trip. Since they already own a travel wardrobe, they just need to make sure items are clean and ready to pack. For a new destination or a major trip, smart packers often start planning months in advance. They know it is almost impossible to buy tropical resort clothing at home in November when the stores are full of woolens and Christmas merchandise. (Catalog and internet merchants often stock off-season merchandise.)

If you are new to travel-wardrobe planning, start thinking about clothing the minute you decide on a destination and a date. Three to six months ahead is not too soon if you need time to shop for a wardrobe that will travel well and may be out of season where you live. Be patient. Building a wardrobe of versatile travel clothing takes time.

How Much Is Enough?

The wardrobe goal for any traveler is to plan for and pack clothes that meet the needs of all planned events, that are comfortable and clean, and that allow you to blend in with the local population — all while taking as few things as possible. The main obstacle is your expectations — a suitcase simply cannot offer the same variety as your closet at home.

Most packing guides stress taking as little as possible; one even suggests taking your old clothes and leaving them behind as you travel. That sends chills to my fashion-loving heart! I take clothing I love so I will look and feel great and have a wonderful time.

How do you decide how much to take? Your answers to the following questions should give you a clue.

1. Is this a fashion trip? ❏ yes ❏ no

If you are going to Paris to tour fashion houses as Marla did, the answer is yes — take everything you need to be beautifully dressed, no matter how many bags it takes. If you are going on an African safari, the answer is no — travel light.

2. Is this a prince/princess trip? ❏ yes ❏ no

If you are staying in five-star hotels with doormen and bellmen the answer is yes — take everything you want since someone else will be carrying it. If you are stopping every night at a different walk-up bed and breakfast, the answer is no — travel light.

To me, traveling light means being able to get around with all my gear by myself. "Light" does not always mean "carry-on." You *can* compromise between bare bones travel and taking the entire closet. I am not happy when my back and arms ache from lugging too much. On the other hand, there are times when I want what I want and am willing to do what it takes to get it there. I use the following rules as my guide when packing to travel light.

Susan's Luggage Laws

1. When you most need help with luggage, there is none.

2. If you can't lift and maneuver your gear by yourself after you've packed it all, edit the contents down to the amount you can manage alone.

3. Two smaller bags are usually easier to manage than one large one.

I learned a lesson when I lived in a tall Victorian house and had to drag large and heavy luggage up one flight of steep stairs to the front door and another flight to the second-floor guest room where I packed: *Always be able to manage your baggage by yourself!* I learned to bounce my bags down the stairs (requires sturdy luggage and lots of packing around fragile contents) and to unpack in the first-floor dining room! To decide how much luggage you can manage by yourself, ask yourself these questions before each trip:

1. How will you get your luggage to and from your car or taxi when you leave home and return?

2. Will you be able to lift your fully loaded bags into your car; will they fit into your car? Will you still have room for yourself and any other expected passengers (and their luggage)?

3. Can you maneuver your bags through a bus/train station or airport? Can you lift them up onto the counter for the ticketing agent to tag for your destination?

4. If your bag is a carry-on, can you lift it over your head to place it in an overhead bin? In today's aircraft, the seats are so close most bags will not go under the seat.

5. At your destination, will you be able to get your bag into your room and still have space for yourself? (I'm thinking of my friend's apartment in New York with its charming but narrow circular staircase going to the charming but small second-floor guest room.)

6. Will you be able to navigate cobblestone streets; Japanese train stations with no escalators or elevators; third-floor walkup bed and breakfasts; or small hotels in Rome? Just because a bag has wheels doesn't mean you will always be able to use them. The key question is, *"Can you actually carry your bags when they are fully loaded?"*

Avoid the "What Ifs"

The greatest sabotage to traveling light is "what if."

"What if I am invited for lunch with the Queen?"

Have you ever been invited before? The possibility is remote but if you are invited, go shopping for the perfect thing to wear.

"What if I am invited to a formal ball while I'm in New York?"

Have you ever been invited to a formal ball on the spur of the moment before? Chances are slim you will be invited this time. If you are, find a formal rental store. The formal wear rental business now offers women's wear, including strapless bras and evening shoes. Your size matters — not all heights and weights can be accommodated.

SMART TRAVEL

Ellen unexpectedly needed a formal gown so went to a Junior League resale shop and found an acceptable dress. She wore it that evening and donated it back to the shop the next morning. How clever; there was no need to pack it around on the rest of her trip!

Remember — if you have planned well and packed smart, you should be able to make do with what you have in your bags. And if you can't make do, you can always rent, buy, or borrow something appropriate for an unexpected event.

Travel Light Wardrobes — His and Hers

What you take on your trip will be very personal but I offer you these two lists as an example of how my husband David and I planned and packed for a recent 14-day trip to Germany during the month of October.

Our itinerary included stops in several different cities for business, followed by a few days visiting family and friends. The trip required taking the train several times plus traveling by car. We packed very light, knowing that European trains allow little time to board and baggage is most often stored in an overhead rack, not checked. We also knew that train stations in small towns sometimes have stairs only (no elevators, escalators or ramps) so carrying our luggage would be necessary. We each took a 22" wheel-aboard suitcase that we checked on the plane but carried elsewhere, plus a small carry-on for in-transit needs.

Although we had done our pre-trip research, the weather was the most difficult factor to contend with during our trip. En route, Fall arrived with a vengeance. It was 10° to 15° cooler than we had anticipated, with frequent rain. But, there was a gift in that — our bags became even lighter as we wore most everything we'd packed just to keep warm! You'll find lists of what each of us took on the next two pages.

David's Packing List

- Navy wool gabardine blazer
  (worn on plane)
- Khaki casual pants
  (worn on plane)
- Red short-sleeved polo shirt
  (worn on plane)
- Purple short-sleeved
  polo shirt
- Beige silk sweater
  (worn on plane)
- Tan wool dress slacks
- Dress shirts —
  3 long-sleeved; could be
  worn with tie or sweater
- 2 ties
- 3 casual shirts —
  2 short-sleeved,
  1 long-sleeved
- Black jeans
- White cotton turtleneck
- 2 cotton tee-shirts —
  1 green, 1 blue
- Long raincoat with liner;
  umbrella (carried on plane)
- Nylon pullover windbreaker
  (carried on plane)
- 2 Hats — 1 wool, 1 cotton
- Gloves (in coat pocket)
- Wool muffler
- Walking shoes
  (worn on plane)
- Cordovan dress loafers
- Pajamas and slippers
- Underwear and socks for
  4 days (time between
  laundry stops)
- Running tights (worn also
  as long underwear)
- Shaving kit
- Coffee mug

*Casual
dress*

*Business
attire*

Susan's Packing List

- Black wool gabardine blazer (worn on plane)
- Matching black gabardine pants
- Black and cream tweed wool pants
- Black cotton leggings (worn on plane)
- White tee-shirt (worn on plane)
- Blue denim shirt (worn on plane)
- Black jeans
- Cream short-sleeved turtleneck
- Black short-sleeved turtleneck
- Black long-sleeved turtleneck
- White long-sleeved shirt
- Red-and-white striped long-sleeved shirt
- Red wool twin sweater set
- Red silk blouse
- 3 scarves
- Costume jewelry
- Long raincoat with liner; umbrella (carried on plane)
- Nylon pullover windbreaker
- Gloves (in coat pocket)
- Black "shopping" shoes (worn on plane)
- Black flats
- Athletic walking shoes
- Nightgown, robe, and slippers
- Underwear and socks for 4 days (time between laundry stops)
- Silk/wool undershirt for warmth
- Cosmetics
- Dual voltage hair dryer*
- Dual voltage immersion heater*
- Mug and instant coffee*

*See "Worthwhile Travel Gadgets" beginning on page 191.

Casual dress

Business/ shopping attire

Every item we each packed was well used. I layered: silk/wool undershirt and black leggings under turtleneck and jeans, topped by denim shirt, red cardigan, raincoat, and gloves and umbrella! David did the same. For a nice dinner with customers I wore the warm undershirt under my silk blouse with the pant suit and added a fabulous scarf and evening costume jewelry. David wore a white shirt and tie with his navy blazer and tan slacks.

Even though the weather was more extreme than anticipated, we were not cold for any long period of time. Getting cold gave us a great excuse to pop into a cozy tavern and sip hot mulled wine with the locals. Our clothes worked well, we had everything we needed, traveling light proved essential for this trip, and we had a fabulous time. Looking back at my packing list for Germany, I realized that I would never wear black every day for two weeks at home. However, it was perfect for the trip. Be sure to read "Planning for the Weather," beginning on page 29.

The real lesson is how you dress at home may be different than dressing for travel. When all is planned and packed, you must be confident that your suitcase contains everything you will need for the trip, even though the selection might be smaller and different than at home.

Nine Ways to Pack Less

Here are nine easy ways to lighten your load that will work for just about any trip you can imagine. Less can be more when you pack the right pieces!

1. **Pack versatile pieces.** Team wardrobe pieces in new combinations to get more mileage out of your clothes on your travels as well as at home. Separates are the most versatile items. Wrinkle-resistant clothes such as dark jeans, khakis, and denim pants or skirts show little dirt and can coordinate with many tops. Learn more about using what you have by reading about "Scarecrowing" on page 44-45. The unisex clothing items shown on the next two pages will give you a head start on your planning.

Pack Versatile Pieces (for men or women)
A perfect wardrobe for a casual, cool-weather trip.

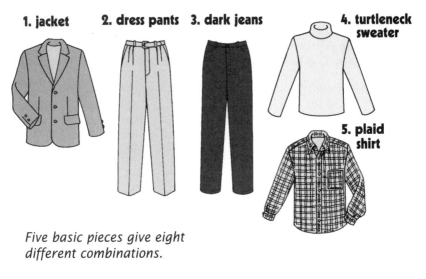

1. jacket   **2. dress pants**   **3. dark jeans**   **4. turtleneck sweater**

5. plaid shirt

Five basic pieces give eight different combinations.

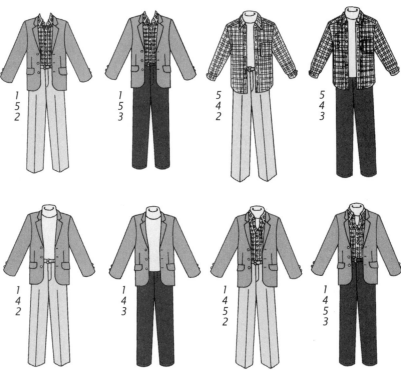

Adding one more piece creates six more outfits.

6. shirt

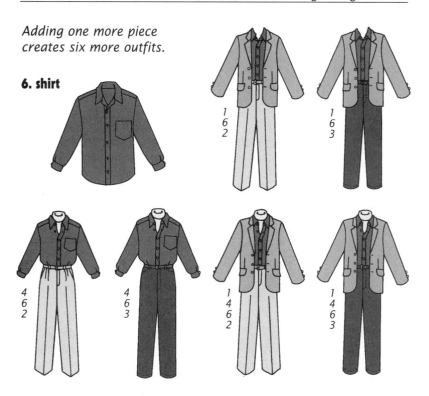

Women can substitute a skirt for pants or jeans, or add it for four more combinations.

7. skirt

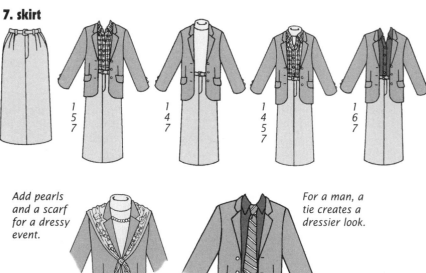

Add pearls and a scarf for a dressy event.

For a man, a tie creates a dressier look.

2. **Plan everything around a basic color.** Choose medium to dark, neutral solid colors for your main wardrobe pieces so each item will go with everything else. Prints are less versatile but hide wrinkles and soil as do darker colors. My personal choice is black. Sophisticated for city wear, black doesn't show wrinkles or soil; it can be worn all day and it can be dressed up for evening. I add color accents: a red sweater, a denim shirt, a gold metallic top; all change the mood and add variety. Other good neutrals are gray, navy, brown, tan, khaki, taupe, and burgundy. Choose one that you're comfortable wearing and that interchanges with other pieces you already own.

3. **Plan to wear each item several times during the trip — and no whining!** Don't be like my mother who wants to wear a completely different outfit every day of her trip. Unless you are on a group tour, it is unlikely that you will be seeing the same people every day. Even when you do, they will admire your wardrobe creativity.

4. **Pack fewer pieces if you will have access to laundry facilities** partway through your trip. Seven changes of underwear will do for a 14-day trip if you have a laundry stop halfway through your trip. Prices for hotel laundry and dry cleaning can be exorbitant and may not fit your timing. Changing hotels every night limits your options to hand washing or finding an all-night, self-service laundry. I pack hand-washable, drip-dry items that require no ironing. That way I can pack two pair of underwear — one to wear and one to wash. I also choose clothing that can be worn several times without cleaning.

5. **Plan to double up!** Plan to pack versatile items that can do double duty, such as:

- A denim shirt that can also be a light-weight shirt jacket

- A pretty blouse that can also be worn as a jacket over a camisole or silk tee shirt

- A long tee-shirt that can serve as a night-gown, robe, beach cover-up, dress, or a top over tights

- Silk or high-tech-fiber long underwear that can be layered under clothing for daytime warmth, worn as sleep-wear, or layered under a long sleep shirt — you're ready for the Arctic if need be

- Exercise tights or leggings with a tee-shirt that you can use for working out, sleeping, lounging, or layering for warmth under pants or dresses

- Women's tank swimsuit that can do double duty as a top with a skirt or pants

- Men's lightweight nylon or Supplex® shorts that can also be worn as a swimsuit

- Dark pants to wear casually with a tee-shirt by day and dressed up with a coat and tie or dressy top for dinner

Dark pants go from day to dinner.

6. **Take more tops than bottoms.** Every top should go with every bottom. Tops weigh less and take less room than bottoms. For those of us who spill and spot more than others, tops are easier to launder.

27

7. **Choose thin items over bulky ones.** Two thin sweaters (turtleneck + cardigan) are as warm as one bulky sweater but are more versatile and take less space. Bulky items such as a heavy coat or jacket can be worn on the plane, but what if you have to pack these — where will they fit?

Thick items take up more space than thin ones.

8. **Select simple, narrow, and shorter pieces** to cut down on bulky folds and save on space. They will also wrinkle less.

This takes up less space.

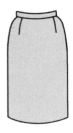

These take up more space.

9. **Take no more than three pair of shoes,** including those you plan to wear while traveling. (Yes, I said just three!) Shoes are bulky and heavy so limit them. My black clothes work with an attractive and comfortable pant shoe and a dressier sandal, flat, or mid-heel, depending on my destination and the season. The shoes I pack are never new and they are always the most comfortable shoes in my closet. Travel usually involves a lot of walking and I know I will not have a good time if my feet hurt. (See "Shoes for Everyone" on page 58.)

Planning for the Weather

There is no bad weather, only inappropriate clothing.

Even though you've done your pre-trip research, the weather can play tricks and turn out to be other than what you expect. For example, you've planned a trip to New England to see the fall colors and you're watching the weather. It has been sunny and clear with temperatures hovering between 60-65°F so you've packed accordingly. However, as your plane lands the weather changes to rain and 50°F. What do you do? Many of my survey respondents said, "Shop, of course."

I say, "Layer." Open your suitcase and put on more layers of clothing until you are warm. If the weather changes from cool to warm, one of the shirts you packed should be a short-sleeved shirt. Simply add or subtract clothing that you have with you until you are comfortable. It is all about packing the right layers.

BASIC OUTFIT	TO BE WARMER	TO BE WARMEST
shirt pants blazer	shirt pants blazer **PLUS** *turtleneck* *sweater*	shirt pants blazer turtleneck sweater **PLUS** *silk underwear top and bottom* *windbreaker/raincoat* *hat* *gloves* *shawl or scarf*

Surviving Cold Weather

I always pack a few small items that make a big difference in my comfort if the temperature drops. I call these "in-case" items — in case I need them they are there. If they stay packed in the bottom of the suitcase for the duration of the trip, I am pleased. My list is on the next page.

"In-Case" Items for Cold Weather

- Long underwear top and bottom made of silk or high-tech fabric (see "Carefree Travel Fabrics" beginning on page 67).
- Warm socks. Take two pair, one to wash and one to wear.
- Turtleneck that can be layered by day or worn for sleeping
- Hat. Wool or polyester fleece are the warmest choices.
- Gloves have amazing warming power.
- Scarf or muffler, or large wool shawl for women. Wear the shawl under or over a coat for an additional warm layer. You can also use it for a light wrap during the day or for an elegant evening wrap, depending on your fabric choice.

Staying Dry in Wet Weather

Don't let wet weather spoil an otherwise perfectly planned trip. Pack these "in case" items to keep you dry in drippy weather.

"In-Case" Items for Wet Weather

- Water-repellent raincoat or jacket, or a fold-up plastic raincoat or poncho
- Rain hat
- Lightweight, collapsible umbrella
- Extra shoes and socks to wear while the wet ones dry (Spray shoes, including the soles, with waterproofing silicone spray before departure.)

Dressing for Hot Weather

If you're not used to it, hot weather can make you cranky and uncomfortable. The most important tip for handling hot weather is *"Be prepared."* Watch the weather and understand what the numbers mean. In dry Phoenix, 95°F may feel quite comfortable. The same thermometer reading in Bangkok can be unbearable due to the high humidity. (See "What About the Heat Index?" on page 16.) Here is an example of how to prepare for the heat.

Cool But Covered Clothing

modest neckline
and sleeves

cool,
woven-
fabric
shirt

comfortable
loose waistlines

sun
hat

Shorts
are okay
in some
countries.

longer
length
skirt

comfortable
walking sandal

If you're Bangkok-bound in June, you can count on an average daily high of 90°F with 90% humidity and 6″ of rain for the month. What should you take?

- **Select clothing that fits loosely and breathes,** allowing air to circulate. Pants and skirts with elastic or drawstring waistlines are cool and comfortable as are dresses without waistlines. For women, loose-fitting dresses are cooler than pants or shorts and a shirt. Divided skirts are also cooler and more modest than fitted pants or shorts. Thin, woven fabrics breathe better than knits and are cooler.

- **Choose underwear of cotton or a moisture-wicking fabric.**

- **Pack moisture-wicking socks if you must wear closed shoes.** A cooler alternative is to wear a comfortable walking sandal.

- **Read "Carefree Travel Fabrics"** beginning on page 67 to learn about cool fabrics that absorb perspiration (cotton, linen, rayon) and cooling synthetics that will wick perspiration away from your body.

- **Save light colors for hats and tops to minimize laundry,** even though lighter colors reflect sun and heat better than dark ones.

- **Take extra clothing.** You will perspire more and want to change clothes often. You'll need to do laundry more frequently and things will take longer to dry in high humidity. Many travelers think they can simply buy inexpensive extra clothing at their destination if necessary, but in many countries the local people are so small that affordable clothing available in the markets will not fit.

- **Read "Worldwide Wardrobing"** beginning on page 36. No matter what the temperature, in some countries the people dress conservatively so shorts and bare tops are not acceptable in most places. Even more revealing clothing is out of the question. Some hotels do not allow shorts to be worn in the lobby.

- **Plan to carry a long-sleeved shirt or shawl with you** to wear inside. Buildings are often kept at a frigid temperature to remove humidity.

- **Take sunscreen, a hat with a brim, and mosquito repellent —** all necessities in hot, humid climates.

SMART TRAVEL *Item*

Leave your straw hat at home. It's awkward to carry and difficult to pack. Instead, buy an inexpensive one at your destination and leave it there when you depart. Or, check out folding or rolling straw hats available in many travel clothing catalogs.

SMART TRAVEL *Item*

Special sunblock clothing with an SPF of 30+ is available for those who really shouldn't be in the sun but want to be outside. A typical summer shirt provides only an SPF 5-9, so specially treated sunblock clothing provides great added protection. Shirts, pants, hats, and jackets are among the many items available. Go to www.skincancer.org and look for "sun-protective clothing" to find retailers.

Managing Temperature Variations

polo shirt

You are planning a trip to Arizona in May. Your first stop is Phoenix where the temperature will be in the 90s by day and 60s at night. Your next destination is the Grand Canyon with daytime temperatures in the 70s, dropping to the 40s at night. How can you pack one wardrobe that will meet the demands of this wide variation in temperatures?

woven shirt

shorts

sweater

jacket

long pants (not jeans)

Here's one layering example for either men or women:

To be warm:
polo shirt
woven shirt
sweater
long pants
jacket

To be cooler:
polo shirt
long pants
sweater

To be coolest:
woven shirt
shorts

In my experience, a lightweight woven cotton shirt is much cooler than a cotton knit tee-shirt or a polo shirt. The open weave and looser fit of a woven shirt allows more cooling air to pass by your body. If you must wear a polo shirt in hot and humid weather (playing golf for example), look for a high-tech synthetic fabric that wicks and is more comfortable than cotton. (See "Carefree Travel Fabrics" on beginning on page 67.)

Women who live in hot climates agree that a loosely fitted, body-skimming dress is usually cooler than a top with shorts. Breezes flow under the dress instead of being stopped by a hot sticky waistband. A simple dress can be very versatile.

A layering example with a dress:

dress   turtleneck   sweater   tee-shirt

tights

To be warm:
dress
turtleneck
tights
sweater

To be cooler:
dress
tee-shirt

To be coolest:
dress

Dressing for Access

On a trip to Thailand, I watched two tourists as they were turned away from touring the Grand Palace in Bangkok because they were improperly dressed. This site is both a temple *and* the home of Thailand's highly revered King; the couple was turned away because they were "not showing proper respect" in the attire they had chosen for the heat and humidity — shorts, tank tops, and rubber thongs. Unfortunately they hadn't done their travel homework, which would have told them that proper attire for the palace includes a shirt with a collar and sleeves, long pants or a longer skirt, and closed shoes. The palace guards might have made an exception if they had violated only one part of the dress code, but they did not comply in any way. They were denied entrance to something they had gone halfway around the world to see — an easily avoidable tragedy.

Americans are the most casually dressed people in the world. If we want to fit in we must dress up more than we do at home. People in other countries dress more formally, more conservatively, and with greater modesty than Americans, no matter how hot the weather. Shorts and tank tops are OK at home but are considered "beach attire only" in much of the rest of the world. Deni reminds us that there are still places that require women to wear skirts or dresses.

Packing Universally Appropriate Attire

Here's a handy list of the most universally appropriate travel clothing that will get you in (practically) anywhere. Don't be caught in a foreign country without appropriate clothing if you want to see everything and get the most out of your trip.

Go-Anywhere Wardrobe

1. **Shirt with a collar**
2. **Shirt with sleeves**
3. **Modest necklines for women**
4. **Long pants such as khakis**
5. **Bermuda-length, just-above-the-knee shorts**
6. **Skirts or culottes that fall well below the knee**
7. **Sport coat or blazer**
8. **Comfortable walking shoes or sandals**

Universally Appropriate Travel Clothing
You can't go wrong with these!

1. Shirt with a collar.
Tee-shirts are not as go-anywhere as polo shirts.

2. Modest necklines for women

3. Shirt with sleeves.
Sleeveless styles are not as acceptable for either women or men.

4. Skirts or culottes that fall well below the knee

5. Bermuda-length, just-above-the-knee shorts *if you must wear shorts. Short shorts are OK for only small children.*

6. Long pants such as khakis

7. Sport coat or blazer

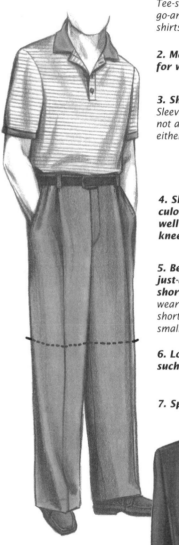

8. Comfortable walking shoes or sandals *(not athletic shoes)*

If your suitcase contains the items shown at left, it is a simple matter to look around and see what other people are wearing, then dress as they do. I usually put on a very conservative outfit the first day in a new place while I observe what the local people are wearing and learn what I should wear to blend in.

Long pants (and longer skirts) are the key, as well as dressing to keep the chest, shoulders, and arms covered. There is no difference in comfort or packability between wearing a pair of jeans and a pair of khakis; I can go practically anywhere in khakis but may be denied entrance wearing jeans. A tee-shirt is no more comfortable than a knit polo shirt, but a polo can go more places. Skirts are more comfortable than pants in most weather. It makes sense to pack the items that will allow me to go anywhere.

SMART TRAVEL

Peggy F., who lived in Germany, and Marcy, who lived in Switzerland and Germany, stress that Europeans wear darker colors. Neutrals such as gray, beige, brown, black, and navy are worn more and are more acceptable than brights in much of the world. Softer, more muted tones will help you keep a low profile.

Tricks to Make Clothes Work

Even if you do a great job of travel research before you leave, there's always a chance that you won't have the perfect piece of clothing for a particular situation — or that your day may require different attire for different events. Use the following strategies to make what you did pack work for you.

1. For women: Tuck a large scarf into your purse. If the church or temple you want to tour requires a covered head or covered shoulders, simply tie on your scarf.

Liz was touring Greece on a moped and found wearing longer shorts more practical than a skirt. She suggests that if you carry a scarf large enough to be worn as a sarong, you can create a long skirt to tie over your shorts or short skirt. This may not get you into the Ritz for tea, but it will create a more modest appearance as required by churches and temples. A second smaller scarf may be required to cover your head and shoulders.

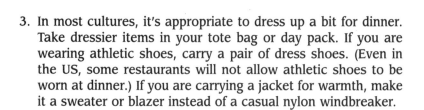

2. Several manufacturers make pants for both men and women that become shorts by zipping off the legs. Keep the legs with you and zip them on if long pants are required. (Go to www.exofficio.com or see Resources, page 237, for travel clothing retailers.)

3. In most cultures, it's appropriate to dress up a bit for dinner. Take dressier items in your tote bag or day pack. If you are wearing athletic shoes, carry a pair of dress shoes. (Even in the US, some restaurants will not allow athletic shoes to be worn at dinner.) If you are carrying a jacket for warmth, make it a sweater or blazer instead of a casual nylon windbreaker.

CHAPTER 5

Packing Perfectly

It's time to get serious — what will work and what won't, versus what I want and what I love.

You've done your planning, decided on your travel style, and have thought about the amount of luggage that you will take. Now it's time to select exactly what will go into your bag for your upcoming trip.

Use What's in Your Closet!

The perfect travel wardrobe is made up of things you like to wear — things that are comfortable, versatile, and appropriate for your destination. If you take things you love, you'll feel good about packing less. After you've searched your closet for things you already own, you can make a shopping plan to supplement and fill out your travel wardrobe needs. To jump-start your closet search, read through the clothing packing lists on page 50.

Look in your closet for tried and true travel performers, or for things that have the potential to become so. Look for:

1. **Easy-care, wrinkle-resistant fabrics.** Easy-care clothing that drips dry after a quick swish in the bathroom basin and requires no ironing is best. Things that can wait for professional dry cleaning when you return home also qualify. Choose things you know still look good at the end of a long day. If something usually looks wrinkled by lunch, do not travel with it. (Also see "Carefree Travel Fabrics," beginning on page 67.)

2. **Knit or stretch-woven fabrics.** Generally, knits (tee-shirt fabric) wrinkle less and are more comfortable than woven fabrics (man's dress shirt fabric) because they have built-in stretch. Some new woven fabrics have stretchy Lycra® added, making them more comfortable, less prone to wrinkles, and great for traveling in comfort and style.

3. **Loose-fitting clothing.** Our bodies expand in flight — and often on vacation. You will not have a good time if your waistband is tight today and you're on your way to the best restaurants in San Francisco. A looser garment is more traveler-friendly than constricting, fitted styles.

Look for:

elastic waist

relaxed shape with undefined waistline

drawstring waist

4. **Clothing with pockets,** particularly interior zippered ones. Pockets are the handiest and most secure storage possible. If you don't own clothing with interior pockets, consider buying some. Look for them in jackets, shirts, pants, shorts, and skirts.

SMART TRAVEL *Item*

Several travel-oriented catalogs feature jackets, shirts, pants, and skirts with numerous zippered inside pockets for secure storage while traveling. Check out "Travel Clothing" in Resources, page 237, for choices for women and men.

Create a Packing Area

Designate a space where you can assemble the items you are considering for your trip. A spare bedroom is ideal, but you may need to be creative if space is at a premium. In addition to my "trip shelf" for travel-only items plus things I'm gathering for the next trip, I use an "over-the-door" rack or a portable rolling rack set up in the guest room, which has now become "Packing Central."

1. Separate out the travel wardrobe possibilities from what's in your closet. Put things out where you can see them so you can add, subtract, and coordinate.

2. Keep adding to this selection with clothing, accessories, and shoes. (See "Finishing Touches" beginning on page 51.) Check each item and take care of any needed repairs and cleaning. When you think of something you want to take, place it in "Packing Central" or make a note to yourself to do it as soon as possible.

3. To pull your wardrobe together, do your fashion homework using a trick from the pros. Make an idea bulletin board with magazine and catalog clippings of looks that you like and can imagine yourself wearing. Now you have some creative new ideas for how to put your pieces together and some possible additions to your travel wardrobe.

Karen places accessories for each outfit in a plastic bag and hangs it on the same hanger with the garment. When it is time to pack she has everything ready to go; no more forgotten earrings or matching belt.

Edit What You've Selected

Now it's time to get serious about what you will really put in the suitcase. Follow the steps below to create outfits that will work for your trip with the minimum number of pieces.

1. **Make "scarecrows" of possible wardrobe combinations.** A scarecrow is a completely accessorized outfit placed on your bed as if it were on your body. You can quickly experiment with changes without even taking the time to try things on. This is how to find new ways to wear clothes already in your closet and to decide on pieces to add.

   If you have a printed bedspread, cover your bed with a plain sheet to eliminate distractions. Put all the clothing and accessory items from "Packing Central" on the bed, leaving an empty place at the end. To create a scarecrow in the empty space:

   • Start with a basic pair of pants or skirt and jacket.

   • Add a shirt, blouse, tee-shirt, or sweater.

   • Accessorize with scarves or ties, costume jewelry, and shoes (remember that you should plan to take only three pair of shoes, including the ones you will wear traveling).

   • Interchange other bottoms, tops, and accessories to increase the versatility.

   • Change this outfit from casual to dressier using other pieces and accessories.

A Scarecrow

Next, try on the combinations that look like possibilities and check the final product in a full-length mirror. How does it look? Does this outfit feel comfortable? When you find a winning combination, write it down or take an instant photo so you won't forget. Include these with your "itinerary calendar."

2. **Review "Nine Ways to Pack Less"** beginning on page 23 and make sure that your selections follow those guidelines. For example, can you wear every top with every bottom?

3. **Fill in the spaces on your "itinerary calendar"** with combinations from the scarecrow experience. Do you have enough for all activities planned for the trip or do you need to shop for a few pieces to complete your wardrobe? Shop early; you will want to test wear and scarecrow these new pieces too.

I always wear a new item before taking it on a trip to make sure it is comfortable and will perform as I intend. What good is that new pair of pants if it looks awful after one wearing when I planned to wear it several times? If I don't like something at home, it is simple to open the closet and make another choice. If I'm not happy with a wardrobe piece from my suitcase, I have few, if any, alternatives.

4. **Do a trial packing with the suitcase you chose for the trip** to see if everything will fit. If not, pare down or choose another bag. If it fits, good for you!

5. **Unpack and hang your clothes until it's time to pack** for your trip.

Style to Go

Personal style is how you make fashion your own. If I show a tailored blazer and your style is a soft jacket, pack that instead. Do not differentiate your travel wardrobe from your daily wardrobe. Remember, it is best to choose items you love from your own closet for a trip. You know how they perform, they fit well, and you feel good in them. Wearing what you love is one of the keys to traveling comfortably.

As you add new items to your regular wardrobe, follow the guidelines for clothes that travel well. Study the fiber and fabric information on pages 67-77 and apply those tips to selecting wardrobe additions. You'll soon have a day-to-day wardrobe that reflects your personal style and packs like a dream.

Travel-friendly clothing does not have to be expensive. I am delighted by the increasing availability of great travel clothes in all price categories.

Listed below are some companies that gear their clothing to a carefree lifestyle, which is what travel is really all about. Some resources label an item "perfect for travel," but don't limit yourself to only those. Although the list is made up of nationwide stores and catalog merchants, be sure to check out your favorite neighborhood shops, discount stores, and department stores as well. Ethnic clothing shops that sell fuss-free, natural-fiber clothing are another great resource.

Travel-oriented mail-order catalogs and on-line retailers also offer a wide array of choices in high-performance travel wear. The selection is generally conservative in style, but it pays to look at these purveyors of basics. The "Indispensable Black Travel Dress™" from TravelSmith is definitely basic, but it will go around the world in a tote bag without a wrinkle. It only requires your personal sense of style. (Turn to "Resources," page 237, for complete shopping information.)

For Travel Classics:

- Columbia Sportswear ††
- Duluth Trading ††
- Eddie Bauer® †† ◊
- Ex Officio ††
- Lands' End †† ◊
- L.L.Bean Traveler †† ◊
- Magellan's® †† ◊
- Norm Thompson †† ◊
- Orvis ††
- Patagonia® ††
- Sahalie ††

For Fashion to Go:

- Bloomingdale's by Mail †† ◊
- Chico's®
- Coldwater Creek® ◊
- J. Crew †† ◊
- J. Jill ◊
- Macy's by Mail †† ◊
- Neiman Marcus †† ◊
- Nordstrom †† ◊
- Saks Fifth Avenue †† ◊
- TravelSmith †† ◊
- Weekenders ◊

†† = men's and women's
      clothing
◊ = extended size range of
      petite through larger sizes

Susan's TRAVEL WEAR SEWING TIPS

If you sew, you can make some great pieces to fill out your travel wardrobe. I choose to sew when:

- I need a simple three-piece outfit in a travel-friendly fabric that is perfect for mix-and-match and what I want isn't available ready-made. Time spent sewing: 8 hours or less.

- I can't find the perfect blouse in an easy-care fabric that coordinates with my travel wardrobe. Time spent sewing: 3 hours or less.

- No amount of shopping produces a pair of pants that fit in the fabric I want. Time spent sewing: 3 hours or less.

- I find a fabric that performs perfectly as a travel fabric. In the case of Ultrasuede® fabric, ready-made items generally do not fit my size or my style. Sewing an Ultrasuede jacket or coat gives me the fabric I love in my style and size. Polyester fleece is another ideal fabric for travel layering. Unfortunately, it is available ready-made in athletic shapes and bright colors. I bought lightweight taupe "microfleece" (very lightweight fleece, see page 72 and 73 for fabric information) and plan to sew an elegant cardigan that will be warm and pack small. Again, the perfect fabric in my style and fit.

If you don't sew, but want to have travel clothing made or altered, call your local independent fabric shop and ask them for a dressmaker referral. The Association of Sewing and Design Professionals is a nationwide organization of dressmakers and tailors and there may be a member near you (see "Resources," page 237).

Create Your Packing List

As you test pack your clothes into the suitcase for your trip, make a complete list of the things you are taking. Save this packing list so you can edit and revise it for the next trip. Make two copies, one to leave at home and one to keep with you in your important papers. Now you have a checklist to make sure you repack each item at every stop. In case your bags are lost or the contents damaged, it is essential to have an accurate list for insurance claims. Deni creates and stores her basic list on her computer. When she is preparing for a trip she simply prints out a copy and customizes it for her current destination.

SMART TRAVEL

Bill P. says, "Always use a packing list or your belt is automatically left behind."

As a guide for creating a basic packing list that you can adapt as needed, use the lists provided on the next page and at www.smartpacking.com. As you use this list of clothing categories to create your own personal packing list for each trip, be specific. For example, where I list "tee-shirts" you should itemize by writing in short descriptions of the specific ones you plan to take with you.

3 tee-shirts:
  white crew neck
  blue bateau neck
  yellow sleeveless

SMART TRAVEL

Put the item you forget most frequently at the top of your list. I always forget my slip!

Women's Clothing Categories

Lingerie
bras
camisole
handkerchiefs
nightgown
panties
pantyhose
robe
slip
slippers
socks

Tops
blouses
jackets
sweaters
tee-shirts
turtlenecks
vests

Bottoms
pants
shorts
skirts

Dresses and Ensembles
dresses
suits

Accessories
belts
jewelry
scarves

Outerwear
coat
gloves
hat
scarf/shawl
umbrella

Activewear
athletic shoes
bandanna
exercise wear
rubber thongs
swimsuit/cover-up

Shoes
casual shoes
dress shoes
evening shoes or
  sandals
walking shoes/sandals
work shoes

Men's Clothing Categories

Underwear and Sleepwear
handkerchiefs
pajamas
robe
slippers
socks
undershirts
undershorts

Tops
casual shirts
dress shirts
jackets
polo shirts
sweaters
tee-shirts
turtlenecks
vests

Bottoms
casual pants
dress pants
shorts

Suits

Accessories
belts
jewelry
ties

Outerwear
coat
gloves
hat
scarf/muffler
umbrella

Activewear
athletic shoes
bandanna
exercise wear
rubber thongs
swim suit/cover-up

Shoes
casual shoes
dress shoes
walking shoes/sandals
work shoes

CHAPTER 6

Finishing Touches

Add-on's are the difference between basics and creating a "look." Even on a camping trip, your clothes describe you.

Accessories can make all the difference in how you look and feel in your travel wardrobe. Carefully chosen, they have the power to change the mood from casual to dressy in an instant. Most accessories pack small and don't add much weight, another reason to plan to pack these wardrobe additions.

Accessories for Men

Ties: Unless your trip is exclusively an adventure trip, at least one tie is a good idea. This small item can change a very basic shirt into something suitable for an unexpected event. For example, denim shirt + khakis + tie will pass in many instances. A silk or wool knit tie travels well; the most versatile colors are solids in burgundy, navy, and black.

If your trip includes cities and/or countries where dressy events may occur, don't skimp on ties. Suits take up lots of room, ties almost none. Take more ties than you think you'll need.

SMART TRAVEL *Gadget*

The clear plastic "Tie Caddy™" is a small cylinder that rolls a tie up inside to protect it for packing. Businessmen who must travel with several ties suggest a flat case that holds and protects up to ten ties. These are available at luggage and travel stores or at www.tiecaddy.com.

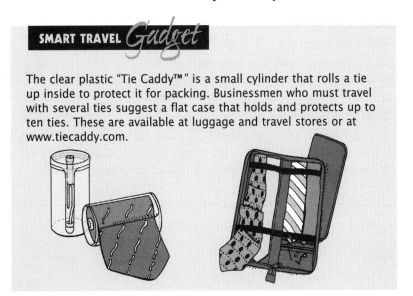

Belts: One casual and one dress belt will meet most needs. Avoid belts with large metal buckles for air travel — they set off the metal detector at security.

If you're traveling in elastic-waist pants or jeans, don't forget to pack your dress belt. David had to spend $100 for a belt in a hotel gift shop so he could attend an early morning meeting, properly dressed, since he hadn't worn or packed one.

Look for reversible belts — one side brown and the other black — for both men and women. What a great idea to cut down on packing weight!

Jewelry: Take as little as possible. A modest watch and a simple wedding ring are the most you should consider wearing. There is simply no secure place for expensive jewelry, including on your body. (See "About Your Jewelry" on page 54.)

Accessories for Women

Belts: Choose simple, versatile styles. A plain leather belt with a matching buckle will coordinate with all jewelry colors. One sporty, one daytime, and one dressy belt are all you'll need for most trips.

Belts with large metal buckles or added embellishments will set off the metal detector at airport security and are impractical for air travel. Since belts are warm, I avoid packing clothing that requires belts when traveling to hot climates.

Scarves: These take up almost no room but have great fashion power. Metallic threads in a scarf add evening glamour. With one 36"-square silk scarf, you can create all the looks shown here.

Fold a square into an oblong:

  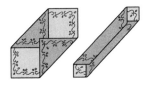

Wrap leaving ends at front or tie as shown:

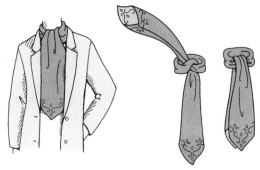

Fold a square into a triangle:

Tie a square knot (right over left, left over right) and move the knot to front, side or back.

Knot center; tie ends to fill in neckline:

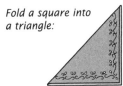  

Fold to oblong; wrap and tie for a belt:

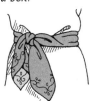

Twist and tie for a belt:

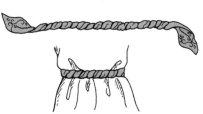

I like to pack a larger scarf to use as a shawl; a 45"- to 50"-square works for me over a dress, jacket, or a coat, and comes in handy as a cover-up on a plane when the cabin temperature is too cool.

Knot ends wrong sides together for a colorful "jacket:"

A smaller 22"- to 25"-square cotton bandanna is really useful for both women and men. Use one for a headband, head wrap, neck scarf, or pocket square. In an emergency, this size is handy as a napkin, clean-up cloth, hand towel or face cloth, sleep mask, dust mask, sweat band, sink stopper, or a purse (tied hobo-style).

Jewelry: Pack as much lightweight costume jewelry as you like. I always pack fake pearls; they are the perfect way to dress up my daytime basics. I just loved having a jewelry store employee compliment me on my "fabulous pearls, Dahling," since they were my plastic ones! A necklace or earrings can change an outfit from casual for day to dressy for dinner. Wear a modest wedding ring (and never take it off) and a simple watch; leave your expensive pieces at home.

ABOUT YOUR JEWELRY — DON'T TAKE ANY CHANCES!

Leave anything of irreplaceable, sentimental, or material value at home. Ignore the impulse to travel with good jewelry; there is simply no secure place for it — including on your body. Please consider that the value of your wedding or dinner ring might equal the lifetime earnings of an individual in the area you are visiting. If this country also puts little value on an individual human life, you could be in danger of losing your life over a single piece of jewelry.

Protect even costume jewelry by packing it in a jewelry pouch or roll. These are available in travel departments and catalogs, but consider these creative alternatives:

- Marta carries her earrings in a plastic film can to protect the posts.

- Sandy likes a hard eyeglasses case for her jewelry.

- Kathleen travels with her stud-type earrings placed through holes punched in a square of Ultrasuede, then tucked into a small, hard-plastic box in her handbag. For an even smaller package, she eliminates the plastic box, tops the Ultrasuede square with a second piece, rolls the two squares with earrings in the middle into a cigar shape and ties with a ribbon. This tiny roll then fits into an inside pocket.

- I have tried many special containers and revert back to a small cardboard box that jewelry comes in from a department store. My current one is 6" x 4" x 1" and holds several pins, necklaces, and numerous pairs of earrings. The structure of the box and the cotton filling inside protect the contents from scratches and crushing. A rubber band keeps the lid in place during travel.

Handbag: One purse for all occasions is the ideal. The perfect bag is small and lightweight (a microfiber bag is excellent), not too casual or too dressy, and contains only the basics required for that day: lipstick, comb, hand sanitizer, tissues, glasses, daily cash, and a credit card or two.

Store other valuables in your room safe or hotel safe, in secure pockets, or in a security wallet worn under your clothes. If you need to carry more, use a tote, a day pack or a waist pack worn in front for safety.

The most secure purse has a zippered top covered with a flap, with a long strap that you wear over the neck and shoulder to the front, bandolier style. (See illustrations on page 216.) Travel retailers offer a good selection of travel purses that meet these criteria.

INSTANT EVENING STRATEGIES

Don't pack special-occasion clothing unless you absolutely must. Use costume jewelry, metallic touches, an evening bag, a great scarf, or a combination of these to transform a simple dark pants and top from a great sightseeing outfit into an elegant evening ensemble.

· Leslie suggests planning for the unexpected by always traveling with small items that carry a big evening punch, such as fake jeweled earrings. Barbara W. gets extra mileage out of her clip-on fake jeweled earrings. She uses them to adorn a neckline or add pizzazz to shoes for an instant evening look.

· Sheila packs a beaded vest that turns her daytime outfit into one dressy enough for dinner.

· Margie automatically takes her long black nylon/Lycra skirt-and-top combo. It packs perfectly and is simple to dress up or down with accessories.

· I travel with a dressy shell top that transforms any solid-color, daytime suit into an elegant one.

Shoes for Everyone

We are so lucky today to have comfortable yet stylish walking shoes. When Aunt Charlotte toured Europe as a teenager in 1921, she went everywhere in heels, stockings, flapper dress, and cloche hat. My feet hurt just thinking about her navigating cobblestone streets in heels!

The wrong shoes can turn a wonderful day of sightseeing into an excruciating nightmare, so it's really important to give some thought to what you will pack and wear. Don't underestimate how much you will be walking, particularly if it's a vacation. The first time I took my sister Nancy K. to New York City, she went home happy but exhausted. She knew she would love New York, but didn't know she would see it all on foot! Walking is often the best way to get up close to what you want to see; occasionally, it is the only mode of transportation available.

Get the Right Shoes

- Think of vacation walking as a form of exercise and get the proper equipment for it. Purchase a pair of good walking shoes far enough ahead of your trip to give you time to break them in. Look for shoes that offer support, shock absorption, and protection. A thick and springy sole will absorb the shocks of walking all day while a leather sole will not. Rubber soles will hold on uneven, slippery, and wet surfaces (wet cobblestones, for example); leather will slip and so will you.

- Plan to spend extra money on quality walking shoes. Visit stores that you might not normally frequent, such as those selling sports shoes and orthopedic shoes. This is a time to choose function and comfort first, styling second.

- Hot weather begs for sandals and there are many styles available that are cool and comfortable and will still support and cushion the feet. As with all walking shoes, thicker rubber soles will add comfort and prevent slipping on uneven or wet terrain. Some sandals may be worn with socks to help span temperatures and eliminate a pair of warmer shoes.

- Shoes are heavy and bulky so plan to take three pair at most, one to wear and two to pack. These must all be comfortable shoes; you will not have fun if your feet are killing you. I take a good looking, very cushioned and comfortable "shopping shoe" (may be a sandal in hot weather), a sporty athletic-type walking shoe, and a flat or mid-heel (or a dressy sandal) for dressing up.

- Because fashion is as important as function to me, I search long and hard for good-looking yet comfortable shoes. On a business trip I substitute a dressier work shoe for the sporty athletic shoe. David travels with Vibram®-soled loafers for daily business wear (he says they are very comfortable), a sporty walking shoe, and a lace-up dress shoe. For casual vacations, he leaves out the dress lace-up and may add a walking sandal for hot-weather destinations.

Good-looking Comfortable Shoes

Casual

Business

Most Casual

- Pack a small shoe horn to help you slip shoes onto swollen feet.

- Add rubber thongs to your shoe list. These inexpensive and flat-to-pack sandals (so flat you don't have to count them into your shoe total!) are perfect for going to and from the pool, beach, or bath down the hall. They're perfect as shower shoes too.

SMART TRAVEL

Sheila suggests creating your own fashionable all-day walking shoes. Purchase a comfortable pair of cushy shoe inserts with arch support or remove them from a pair of shoes you own. Take these inserts shoe shopping and fit them into a fashionable, rubber-soled shoe that is at least one size larger than you normally wear. Walk around the store for a test drive — you should feel like you're wearing your favorite athletic shoes. If not, keep trying until you find a combination that works.

SMART TRAVEL Item

John recommends Kiwi® "Shine Wipes™,"— individual towelettes for an instant shoe shine. They work on all shoe colors. Karen uses a black marking pen to touch up scuffs on black shoes.

FOR HAPPY FEET

- **Change shoes partway through the day.**
Switching shoes changes the pressure points on
your feet, reducing the risk of blisters, unnecessary
discomfort, and swelling.

- **Pamper your feet before putting on different
shoes for the next event on your schedule.**
Soak them in cold water (hot water makes them swell),
give them a quick massage with body or foot lotion, elevate for a few minutes, and then change shoes.

- **Dab your feet with witch hazel** (even over nylon
stockings). It's cool and refreshing.

- **Wear good walking socks** — they help keep feet dry
and minimize bacteria and the risk of infection. Look for
"wicking" socks (see page 74). High-quality, padded
walking socks from the activewear department or a
sporting goods store are a good investment for travel
because they increase the shock absorption and
cushioning effect of your shoe.

- **Include foot powder in your bag** if heading to a hot
climate and use sparingly to help keep your feet dry. I
keep a sample size container of powder in my purse to
reapply during the day.

- **Treat your feet to a soothing footbath** at the end of
a long day of tourist activities. Tuck a few packets of
Johnson's™ Foot Soap in your suitcase — you'll find it
at your drugstore.

CHAPTER 7

Looking Good

Cleanliness comes before Godliness, they say. Make sure you have your "basics" covered.

Frequent travelers speed their packing by keeping a "for-travel-only" toiletries kit always ready to go. Since these items can be heavy and take up lots of space, look for small travel or sample sizes of your favorite toiletries and cosmetics. This is important — over half the weight in a fully packed suitcase can be from these items! Search for double-duty products such as sunscreen and insect repellent in one. Replenish used items immediately after returning home. That way a big part of getting packed is already done the next time you grab your bags to go!

It's important to consider the "what ifs" when fitting out your toiletries kit, particularly when traveling internationally. I hate wasting my tourist time looking for contact lens solution in a strange city or waking up in the middle of the night needing the aspirin I forgot to pack! On the other hand, some people think finding toothpaste in Tibet is part of the adventure. I say, go prepared — create your own customized packing list, using the one on page 66 as a starting point. (See page 201 for must-have items for your traveling medicine chest.)

The Basics

In addition to moisturizer, deodorant, shaving supplies, and hair care products (all in sample sizes), these are the basics (a complete packing list is at the end of this chapter):

1. **Cotton balls, cotton swabs.** Look for small prepacks in the sample size bins of drug/variety stores or pack into snack-sized self-sealing plastic bags.

2. **Insect repellent.** Unless it is the dead of winter, you should pack it. If you're headed to a really buggy place or where malaria is an issue, take a small pocket-size stick of insect repellent so you can reapply during the day (I tuck one into my purse). Mosquito spray for clothing and for your room is a good idea too. Buy insect repellents at home — overseas

brands might contain ingredients whose effects could be worse than the bites. (See page 211 for more information.)

3. **Moist towelettes or antibacterial hand cleaner.** This is a must for those times when you cannot find a place to wash your hands.

4. **Panty shields/tampons/sanitary napkins.** Pack a one-day supply for domestic travel — enough to get you to a drugstore. For international travel take a one-month supply. The locally available products may be primitive at best or your favorite brand may be available but expensive.

5. **Sunscreen.** Because I have temperamental skin, I prefer to take a full container of a brand I know so I'll have no unpleasant reactions. Carry a sample size in your day pack or purse for midday reapplication.

6. **Talcum or baby powder.** These are nice in hot and sticky weather. In tropical places I carry a sample size to reapply midday.

7. **Tissues.** Small packets are indispensable. I line the bottom of my suitcase with them so I have plenty to use — for toilet paper, seat covers, hand towels, napkins, not to mention a drippy nose.

Pack Them with Care

It's no fun to arrive at your destination and find that shampoo has leaked all over your clothes. Following are some take-the-worry-away ideas for packing toiletries and cosmetics.

• Roz reminds us to never pack prescription drugs in checked baggage. These should be in your carry-on in their original containers, especially for international travel. The container should show your name, doctor's name, and a description of the contents. (Drug laws in some countries are very harsh!) If your baggage is delayed, you can remain on your prescription schedule *if* you have it with you.

• If your favorite products aren't available in travel sizes, buy small plastic bottles with screw tops at your drug, luggage, or travel store. Refill as needed.

SMART TRAVEL Tip

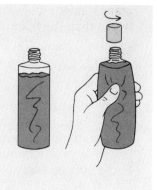

Don't fill bottles full, and if they are full, use some of the product before packing. Changes in air pressure during air travel cause the contents to expand and leak. This can also happen if you simply drive from sea level to a higher altitude. Fill the container almost full, squeeze to remove as much air as possible, and screw the cap on tightly.

- If you're afraid the container will leak, wrap the top with masking tape. Pack pump dispensers and aerosol cans in self-sealing plastic bags.

- Look for a toiletry case large enough to hold your necessities but small enough to fit into your suitcase or carry-on bag. Two smaller containers may be easier to pack than one large one.

- I carry my make-up plus a few basics in a small, clear plastic bag tucked into my carry-on bag. If my luggage and I do not connect, I can still brush my teeth and put on my make-up. I pack my other toiletries in freezer-weight, self-sealing plastic bags in my checked baggage. These bags aren't glamorous, but they can be tucked into open spaces so pack small. I divide things so I have a "take-to-the tub" bag (shampoo, conditioner, face soap, etc.) and my "drugstore" bag (medications, etc.).

Lisa divides her cosmetics into three plastic bags: hair products, face and skin products, and make-up. To minimize bathroom clutter, Pati packs one bag with morning things, a second for her nighttime routine.

SMART TRAVEL Security Update

The TSA (Transportation Security Administration) recommends packing cosmetics and toiletries in checked luggage and now requires following "3-1-1" for carrying on these items:

3= 3 ounce (100 ml) or smaller containers of liquids or gels

1= 1quart-size (1 liter) clear plastic, zip-top bag to hold the 3-oz containers

1= 1 bag only per traveler placed in the security bin for screening.
For more information go to www.smartpacking.com or www.tsa.gov.

SMART TRAVEL *Gadget*

A toiletries bag with a hook at the top frees up limited bathroom counter space. Simply hang it on the shower rod, towel bar, or bathroom door.

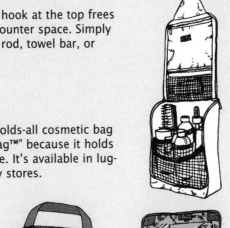

Judith swears by her holds-all cosmetic bag called the "Freedom Bag™" because it holds everything in one place. It's available in luggage and travel supply stores.

- Ruth says a travel magnifying mirror for applying make-up is a necessity. In some hotels, the bathroom light is so bad she stands at the window to put on her make-up using the hand mirror. Nancy K. loves her 5X travel mirror. Look in travel and luggage stores.

- Towels in some hotels leave much to be desired. Often they are small and there are rarely enough. In some countries no washcloth is provided. You may want to pack your own — see page 156 for some suggestions.

Packing List

Below, in alphabetical order, are the things you won't want to forget. Customize this list to meet your specific needs. A printable version is available at www.smartpacking.com.

Body lotion

Cotton balls, cotton swabs

Dental Supplies:
dental floss, mouthwash, toothbrush and toothpaste

Deodorant

Facial Care:
cleanser, moisturizer, toner

Feminine hygiene products

Hair Care:
brush, comb, curling iron, hair dryer, hair rollers/ hot rollers, shampoo and conditioner, hair spray

Insect repellent

Lip balm

Magnifying mirror

Medications/prescription drugs

Moist towelettes or antibacterial hand cleaner

Make-up

Perfume

Shaving Equipment:
after-shave lotion, electric shaver, razor and spare blades, shaving cream, styptic pencil

Shower cap

Sunscreen

Talcum powder or baby powder

Tissue packets

Washcloths and/or towels

CHAPTER 8

Carefree Travel Fabrics

How important is it that you show up wrinkle-free?
Cancel concern by choosing fabrics wisely.

New fabric innovations and airline carry-on luggage restrictions have created a booming business for travel clothes. In the past we had clothing made of natural fibers. It was comfortable to wear but often difficult to pack. Servants put many layers of tissue paper around Madame's gowns as they were packed into steamer trunks for "the crossing." Today, with the right fabrics, we can roll up a Supplex dress, tuck it into the corner of a wheel-aboard suitcase, and expect it to look presentable upon arrival.

Because we all have different lifestyles and travel styles, there is no single best fabric. With some basic fiber and fabric knowledge, however, you will know how to select the best clothes for you and your trip.

For example, I own two pair of khaki pants. One pair is 100% cotton and at the end of the day looks pretty lived in, so I wash and iron it after each wearing. The second pair is 100% cotton with a "wrinkle-free" finish so I can wear it several times and still look fresh. Now, which pair should I choose for travel? Both are cotton and comfortable, but the one that requires less care and can be worn more before it needs attention is the obvious choice. Choosing the wrinkle-free pair means I don't have to pack as many pairs of pants.

Be Fiber Savvy

You'll be a better shopper if you know some basic information about the fibers from which clothing is made and what you can expect from each one during normal wear and maintenance.

A Little Fiber Terminology

Blends are made of two or more fibers, selected for their best features to make an even better fabric.

Finishes are added to the surface of a fiber or fabric to change the natural characteristics. Finishes are not as long lasting as a characteristic that is a natural feature of the fiber.

FOUR TIPS for Choosing Smart-Travel Fabrics

1. Look in your closet for comfortable clothing you can wear several times before laundering. These fabrics will pack without wrinkling and won't require much care.

2. Choose fabrics with intentional wrinkles — crinkled rayon crepe and gauze are great travel choices.

3. Whenever possible, pack easy-care fabrics that you can hand wash and drip dry in your hotel room, or that you can wash and dry in a self-service laundry. Even if you are willing to spend $8.00 to have a dress shirt washed and ironed, hotel laundries may not be able to meet your time schedule.

   Dry cleaning is usually expensive and may take several days. In addition, the quality of cleaning and pressing may be questionable. Pack washables instead or plan to spot clean while on the go (see "Stay Neat and Clean" beginning on page 184 for clothes care) and save dry cleaning for your return.

4. Pack your favorite comfortable things that you know look good on you and that you will be happy wearing many times. If you take new clothing, how will you know if the fabric will perform? You won't know if you can wear it more than once or if you can wash and dry it easily without a lot of fuss.

Traditional Fibers

While you may be familiar with the traditional fibers listed on garment hangtags, you're sure to see some new terms that are the result of high-tech fiber innovations. These often have very positive implications for travel clothing and are included with each traditional fiber.

Wool: Naturally a great insulating fiber, wool can be an all-season fabric except in the hottest, most humid climates. Bedouin robes are made of sheer wool and are worn year-round. Wool gabardine and wool crepe are wrinkle-resistant and resilient; if they do wrinkle a bit, the wrinkles hang out. Wool is durable, and so makes a practical business suit that can mix and match with other business and casual items. A thin wool sweater makes the perfect layering piece in any climate. "Merino" wool is popular today because this long silky fiber from the merino sheep produces lightweight and warm wool clothing that packs small.

New engineering has produced wool that can be machine washed and dried. Lycra spandex is now blended with wool and many other fibers for added comfort stretch and wrinkle recovery.

Cotton: Cotton is another seasonless travel favorite. Cotton jeans, khakis, tee-shirts, turtlenecks, and sweaters are easy-care, packable pieces. They are all more carefree when made of a blend of cotton and polyester because they will resist wrinkling and wash and dry more easily.

Wrinkle-resistant finishes applied to 100% cotton fabrics cut down on wrinkling. They usually come out of the dryer requiring little or no pressing, making a good travel fabric even better. Lycra/cotton blends resist wrinkles and are more comfortable.

Linen: Cool and comfortable even in the hottest, most humid weather, linen has only one drawback — it wrinkles. Tell yourself that wrinkles are fashionable and you love them, or choose another fabric. Linen requires tedious ironing after washing, so dry cleaning is easier.

Linen is often blended with other easy-care fibers to create fabrics that wrinkle less and require less maintenance. "Washed" lightweight linen with obvious wrinkling that is supposed to be "the look" is also easier to care for. These innovations have brought linen back into popularity and to OK travel status, but you will need to develop a love for wrinkles if starched and pressed is your style.

Silk: Often thought of as a luxury fiber, silk can be a durable and wrinkle-resistant travel fabric. It is insulating and warm yet lightweight. Silk long underwear is a good example. Look for heavier weight, textured silks and silk knits for superb travel performance and fashionable good looks for any season. Leave lightweight, flat-weave, dry-clean-only silks at home — they will wrinkle and require high maintenance.

High Tech
MEETS
Traditional

"Sueded silk" (brushing the surface to create a softer fabric with a suede-like finish) and "washable silk" (pretreating silk to minimize shrinkage) are innovations that result in high-performance yet luxurious travel fabrics.

SMART TRAVEL

Sheila bought black silk palazzo pants for travel because the saleswoman assured her they could be machine washed. Sheila tested the claim and found it to be true. She loves her practical and elegant pull-on pants. They take up little room in her suitcase and she can justify the higher price of designer silk because there are no added dry cleaning costs over the lifetime of the garment.

Synthetic Fibers

Fibers made from a variety of ingredients rather than being harvested from natural sources are called synthetic fibers. Most of these have characteristics that make them great travel fabrics.

Rayon: The first man-made fiber, rayon has been around since 1910. It was produced from wood pulp and was designed to be a substitute for expensive silk. Rayon has remained popular because of its special properties: soft drape, ability to take dye beautifully, silky feel, and moisture absorbency. Rayon is the most absorbent of all the traditional fabrics and so is actually cooler than linen and cotton.

High Tech
MEETS
SYNTHETIC

Tencel® is the brand name for the newest generic fiber, lyocell. Tencel is made from cellulose found in trees and is a close cousin to rayon in both manufacturing methods and fabric properties. It is comfortable to wear, dyes beautifully, is absorbent and cool, has excellent drapability, and can be machine washed and dried. Tencel fibers may be knitted or woven; and they can be blended with other synthetics and natural fibers. This excellent travel fabric might wrinkle, but the wrinkles hang out quickly.

Acetate: One of the earliest manmade fibers, acetate was developed from wood pulp as an alternative to silk. This fiber has excellent drapability and softness, and is absorbent and comfortable with no static cling. It has been widely used as a garment lining.

Acetate blended with stretchy spandex produces the popular women's travel fabric — "slinky knit." This comfortable fabric is figure-flattering, machine washable and dryable, and packs like a dream. Look for "slinky knit" coordinates in travel catalogs, department stores, and women's shops.

Acrylic: Versatile acrylics have been available since the early 50s, most commonly seen in sweaters and knitted fabrics. This fiber has outstanding wickability (see page 74), washes well, and dries quickly.

Acrylic blends beautifully with other fibers and with the introduction of microfibers (see page 73), its popularity in blends has increased.

Nylon: This man-made fiber is exceptionally strong; that's why tires, tents, luggage, parachutes, ropes, and carpeting are often made of nylon. It is easy to wash and quick drying, but its low moisture absorbency makes nylon warm to wear in hot weather — not a good choice for trips to hot, humid locales.

Supplex *is nylon engineered to have the soft touch of cotton with the performance advantages of nylon. Supplex is lighter in weight than standard nylon, and it won't shrink, wrinkle, or fade like cotton. It is breathable as well as odor, wind, and water resistant.*

MicroSupplex *™ is microfiber (see page 73) nylon fiber finer than silk. The resulting fabric is soft, drapable, and feather light. MicroSupplex can be woven into a tight, dense, high-performance fabric that resists wind and weather, wears better than ordinary nylon and breathes well.*

Polyester: It's strong, easily washed, quick to dry, and wrinkle resistant — but it can feel warm in hot weather. Polyester fiber is made into a wide variety of fabric types and it blends well with other fibers. Poly/cotton blends are more durable and wrinkle resistant than 100% cotton and more absorbent and cooler than 100% polyester.

Polyester fleece is made of knitted and brushed polyester yarns. Soft, warm, breathable, and strong, it is machine washable and dryable and needs no ironing. Known for its warmth without weight, polyester fleece is available in microfleece for sweaters, medium weights for jackets, and in heavier weights that can be so high performance they are worn on Everest climbs. Two names seen frequently are Polartec® and Polarfleece®.

Synchilla® fleece, polyester fleece from Patagonia, is made from recycled plastic bottles. This fleece transports moisture away from the body or "wicks" (see page 74), breathes easily, and is machine washable and dryable. Patagonia states each Synchilla garment takes 25 two-liter pop bottles out of a landfill and into productive use.

CoolMax is a polyester fiber designed to move or "wick" perspiration away from the body to the outer layer of the fabric, where it dries fast. CoolMax has the fastest drying rate of any fabric—three times faster than cotton. CoolMax also breathes well. Machine washable and dryable as well as shrink-resistant, it is found in shirts, pants, underwear, socks, and sports bras. There are many trade names for fibers that perform like CoolMax; look for the key words "wicking" and "dry."

DECIPHERING HANGTAGS

Use the following list to help you understand new terms that appear on garment hangtags and in clothing descriptions.

Gore-Tex® is the most durable, waterproof, breathable, and windproof outerwear fabric available. Its membrane contains 9 billion pores per square inch, each 20,000 times smaller than a drop of water, but 700 times bigger than a molecule of water vapor. Outside water can't penetrate these pores, but perspiration can easily escape. It breathes better than other waterproof fabrics.

Hemp, a 5,000-year-old fiber, is making a comeback. It is stronger than cotton and as breathable as linen, but it is softer and more carefree. Hemp is grown without pesticides and made into fiber in an environmentally friendly process. Why have you not heard of hemp before? Because it is made from the fibrous inner bark of the marijuana plant! A special strain grown for textile purposes only has been developed.

Bamboo fabric, made of 100% bamboo pulp fiber, is as soft as silk with an elegant, silk-like drape. An absorbent and wicking fiber, bamboo is comfortable to wear. It is also made into bath towels and bed sheets. Bamboo is a sustainable, rapid-growing fiber grown without the use of pesticides and herbicides.

Soy is an eco-friendly fabric made from a by-product of soybean oil production. Soy oil can be extracted from the soybean and used for food, while the remainder is spun into soy yarn. Soy fiber is marketed as a luxury fabric – "vegetable cashmere" – with a lustrous, soft feel. It is washable and durable.

Wicking fabrics are the key to hot-weather comfort and quick drying with hand laundry (see page 75). Here are some of the high tech fabric names for wicking items you will see when shopping: Capilene®, Cool Max®, Double-Dry by Champion®, Dri-FIT®, Dri-Power®, Dri-Release®, Dryline®, Dry-Tech®, Hydrofil®, Intera®, Polartec® PowerDry®, Thermax®, UnderArmour®, VisaEndurance®.

Teflon® Fabric Protector is a long-lasting stain-resistant finish that can be applied to all fibers. Teflon binds with each fiber to repel stains, forcing oil- and water-based stains to bead on the surface so they can be blotted away. It also allows dust and dry soil to be brushed off. This remarkable new finish does not affect the fabric breathability.

Microfibers are so fine it takes 100 of them to equal one human hair. They can be made from polyester, nylon, rayon, or acrylic and are often blended with other fibers. Microfiber fabrics make excellent travel wear because they are lightweight, durable, wrinkle resistant, easy-care, water repellent, and wind resistant. Microfibers are particularly good for outerwear and bodywear because they wick and breathe.

Be Fabric Savvy

Choosing the right fabrics for your trip is as important as understanding what each fiber contributes to the finished fabric. There are several fabric characteristics that you should understand in order to make wise and comfortable fabric choices.

Woven, stretch-woven and knit fabrics:

Woven fabrics (as in a man's dress shirt) are made by interweaving lengthwise threads over and under crosswise threads at right angles. Woven fabrics generally do not stretch and usually wrinkle more than knitted fabrics. Stretch can be added to woven fabrics by using stretchy spandex yarns.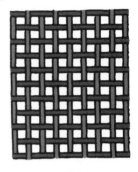

Knit fabrics (as in a tee-shirt) are made on needles, and produce a fabric made up of a series of interlocking loops. Knitted fabrics generally stretch more and wrinkle less than woven fabrics.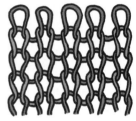

Absorbent fabrics: In the past, we chose fibers that absorbed moisture. The natural fibers — rayon, linen, cotton, and wool — were thought to be the best. Absorbent fibers take moisture away from our bodies and hold it (picture a cotton tee-shirt on a jogger after a long run). The body is cooled as breezes cause evaporation. Imagine the difference between wearing a cotton tee-shirt and a plastic bag on a hot day. The plastic bag traps moisture and heat; the cotton shirt absorbs and cools.

Moisture is absorbed by fabric.

Wicking fabrics: The moisture-wicking process is the high-tech key to comfort. Wicking synthetic fibers have been designed to take perspiration away from the body, transporting it to the fabric surface where it can evaporate. Since perspiration evaporating is how the body cools itself, the faster the fabric spreads moisture to the surface to speed evaporation, the cooler the body feels.

Wicking also keeps your body warm and dry in cold weather by pulling moisture away from the body and preventing cold perspiration from settling on the skin. Fabrics that wick moisture don't absorb moisture so they wash and dry quickly. Cotton absorbs and holds moisture, so drying takes a long time.

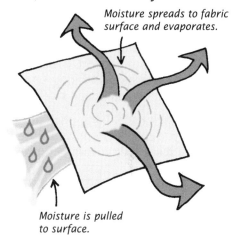

Moisture spreads to fabric surface and evaporates.

Moisture is pulled to surface.

Breathable fabrics: Fabrics that breathe allow air to pass between the threads so that the air evaporates perspiration and cools the body. A plastic bag does not breathe; it traps perspiration and keeps air out. Breathable fabrics do not necessarily absorb or wick moisture, but they still feel cool because they allow air and moisture passage. Supplex is an example of a fabric that doesn't absorb or wick very much, but it breathes to allow air to pass through and so feels comfortable to wear.

Open-weave fabrics also allow air to pass between the threads in the fabric for added comfort.

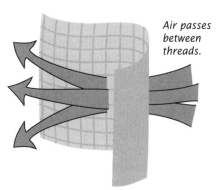

Air passes between threads.

How Does Fabric Affect Packing?

- Knit fabrics are usually more travel friendly than woven fabrics as they wrinkle less and are often more comfortable to wear because they stretch. Knits can be rolled successfully, whereas woven fabrics wrinkle less when carefully folded. Stretch woven fabrics with spandex added behave more like a knit.

- If you are traveling to a hot and humid climate, pack wicking underwear to feel cooler. Wicking items worn next to the skin add to your comfort. A business traveler will be more comfortable wearing a wicking undershirt under a dress shirt, even though it is an added layer.

- To pack really light, pack only three sets of wicking underwear so you can wear one, hand wash one, and have a spare. Wicking fabrics will dry overnight, even in humid climates.

- Supplex pants or skirts pack small without wrinkling, breathe for comfort, and can be hand washed and dried quickly.

- On your way to a cold adventure? Patagonia Capilene long underwear has been worn in Antarctica by explorers who swore their very survival was due to their high tech clothing. This wicking polyester fiber is a great choice for a ski trip or for cold-weather travel.

- A lightweight Gore-Tex jacket can be your most versatile outer layer, spanning temperature extremes based on what you layer under the waterproof and windproof shell. Why pack a bulky winter coat when something smaller will keep you comfortable?

Determine How a Fabric Will Perform

Now that you're armed with lots of information about fibers and fabrics that are travel friendly, you're ready to shop. There are some easy performance tests that you can do to decide if your choice is travel worthy. Here are some things to test.

1. Look at the item. Is it wrinkled on the hanger in the store? Not a good sign. If it wrinkles in the store or wrinkles in your closet, it is a sure thing it will wrinkle in your suitcase.

2. Grab a corner of the fabric and crush it in your hand. Hold it for 30 seconds and let your hand warmth and moisture penetrate the fabric. Now let go. If the fabric does not wrinkle,

it is a good choice. If the fabric wrinkles but the wrinkles shake out after a minute or so, it's a good choice too. If the wrinkles are still there, make another selection; this one will wrinkle in the suitcase *and* when you're wearing it. A rule of thumb: woven fabrics wrinkle more than knits and smooth-surfaced fabrics show wrinkles more than textured ones. Solid colors show wrinkles more than prints.

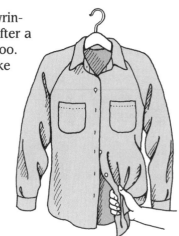

3. Test to see if pants will bag at the knees or a skirt will bulge in the back after just one wearing. Check for shape retention by stretching the fabric between your thumbs and forefingers and holding it for 10 seconds. If the yarns slip apart easily, this could cause stretch and stress on the seams. If there is no yarn shifting and the fabric springs back after stretching, the fabric will hold its shape while being worn. Generally, woven fabrics hold their shape better than knits and synthetic fibers better than natural ones.

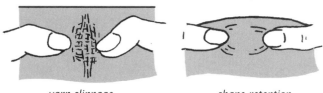

yarn slippage   shape retention

4. Test for fabric "pilling" (those pesky little balls that form on the surface) by turning an inconspicuous corner back on itself and rubbing the layers together. If this produces slight balls or pills, these will occur wherever abrasion occurs during wear — the front of the thigh, pant crotch, and underarm. Pilling does not affect the packability of an item, but it does make the fabric look old and worn before its time.

5. Check for breathability by holding the fabric to your mouth and blowing through it. If no air passes through, the fabric does not breathe and will feel like a plastic bag.

PART II:
PACK
SMART

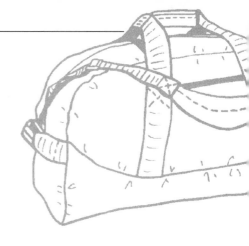

Build a luggage wardrobe so you can choose the best bag for each trip.

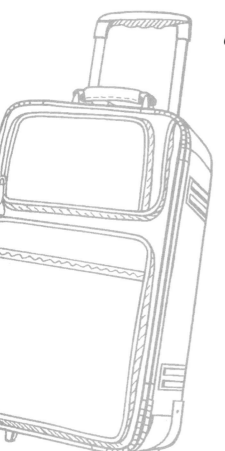

CHAPTER 9

Choosing the Right Luggage

Every day somebody invents a new traveling bag —
but will it work for you? Shop around!

There has been quite a revolution in luggage in the last few years. The biggest seller of ten years ago might well be today's dinosaur. Don't toss your old luggage yet, but now is a good time to look at what you have and decide what you need for the future. Take an inventory of the bags you own and evaluate their condition in a list like the one below:

PERSONAL LUGGAGE PROFILE

Luggage Piece	Dimensions	Condition	Wheels? Yes or No
1. pullman	29 x 20 x 10	old!	no
2. garment bag	28 x 48	unscathed	no
3. carry-on	18 x 12 x 6	ok	no
4. wheel-aboard	22 x 14 x 8	brand new	yes!
5.			

If the condition of any bag is questionable, consider parting with it. If new luggage can be eaten alive by the transportation industry (my biggest fear is seeing the contents of my bag coming around the baggage carousel, one pair of underwear at a time), how will your old and tired bag survive? Keep only those bags that are in good condition. (If you just can't bear to part with an old favorite, consider using it for sports equipment storage in the garage.)

Think about how you travel today. You need luggage that will work for you now — for your current mode of travel. Life changes will alter how you travel, creating different luggage needs. For example, the new college grad who backpacks around Europe will find a favorite backpack less acceptable for business travel but perfect for the next adventure trek.

Forget the idea that quality luggage is a lifetime investment. Travel and technology are changing too fast. Even though Mom's Hartmann luggage set from 1935 is still in great condition, it is a useless antique by today's standards. Why? Too heavy, too big, no wheels. It was designed for train travel where a smiling porter removed the bags from the taxi and carried them onto the train. Now Mom must wheel her own bag — almost everywhere.

Match Your Luggage to Your Travel Style

Answer the following questions to help you decide how you travel so you'll know what luggage will work best for you:

1. What is your travel style today? Check all that apply.

   ❑ Sophisticate   ❑ Resort/sport
   ❑ Casual   ❑ Adventurer

2. How frequently do you travel? Luggage that you use for weekly business travel will require different features than the bag you take on an annual vacation.

   ❑ weekly   ❑ monthly   ❑ 4 trips/year __
   ❑ 2 trips/year ❑ 1 trip/year

3. How long are your trips?

   ❑ overnight __   ❑ 3 nights __   ❑ 5 nights __
   ❑ 1 week __   ❑ 2 weeks __   ❑ 3 weeks __

4. Evaluate the luggage you already own in light of the following questions.

   ❑ Does it meet your needs?
   ❑ Do you have lots of space to store luggage between trips?

   ❑ How large is the car that will transport you and your luggage? Will this bag fit into the trunk or must it go inside the vehicle? Is there room left for the number of passengers who will be traveling?

   ❑ Where do you live — third-floor walkup with no elevator? Where do you pack — in a second-floor bedroom? How will you get your loaded bags in and out of your home?

5. Think about where you are going and how you will get there. Check all that apply.

❑ Public transportation (bus, train, subway) to get to primary mode of transportation

❑ Car, bus, train, or plane, with frequent changes

❑ Car, bus, train, or plane with infrequent changes

6. What is your most common mode of transportation?

❑ car ❑ bus ❑ train ❑ plane
❑ tour bus ❑ cruise ship

Now that you have looked at the luggage you have and have evaluated how you travel, it is time to look at adding new luggage that is right for you.

Consider Luggage Construction

Today, most luggage falls into one of three categories — hard-sided, semi-soft, and soft-sided. Each has its good points and its bad.

1. **Hard-sided bags** protect the contents better than any other bag, making them the best choice for wrinkle-free packing. You can pack fragile items in the center and feel confident that they will arrive intact.

Hard cases are also more water-repellent than any other type. The biggest disadvantage is weight — these bags are heavy even when empty — and they will hold only so much because they are not flexible. However, new polycarbonate luggage changes things — this is one of the lightest and sturdiest plastics around and a 26" bag can weigh as little as 7.3 pounds! Most close with a zipper instead of a clasp, and some expand as much as 2".

2. **Soft-sided bags** are lightweight, fold flat for storage,
and can usually be coaxed into
expanding to hold one more
thing (every bag does have its
limits). Available in many
shapes and sizes, soft-sided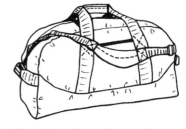
bags are the most flexible and resilient but don't do much
to protect contents from outside impact. They are best for
casual trips and carrying bulky gear when wrinkle-free clothing and fragile items aren't an issue. I find them the very best
for car travel and for private boat trips (not cruises).

3. **Semi-soft luggage** has either a rigid frame
or a firm but flexible frame. The soft top
and bottom are slightly expandable. The
popular wheel-aboard case is an example
of a semi-soft bag. The frame provides
some of the benefits of a hard-sided
bag, such as wrinkle-free packing, without the weight. This type of bag will
protect contents from outside impact
(although not as well as a hard-sided
bag) while retaining some flexibility. I
find these bags very practical for
trips where I must handle my own
luggage. The combination of lightweight
+ wheels + stable frame works well for me.

About Wheels

Built-in wheels or a separate luggage cart (wheelies) that take
the "lug" out of luggage are a necessity for today's traveler. If
you are buying new luggage, insist on wheels. Wheelies are less
convenient than built-in wheels but preferable to struggling,
particularly when traveling with heavy bags.

Know the Luggage Trends

There have been many changes in luggage due to new strict security regulations for all transportation types and newly enforced
airline rulings for checked baggage.

- Strict airline enforcement of bag size and weight limits has forced travelers to pay attention. (See page 94 for details). Rather than traveling with one large, oversized, and overweight bag, pack into two smaller bags that will pass airline rules.

- Lightweight, high-performance luggage is readily available — don't waste packing weight on old, heavy bags. Weigh your old bag and compare to new, high-tech luggage.

Tutto® luggage (see Resources, page 239) offers an innovative design that collapses for storage, a great choice for apartment dwellers and cruise passengers. Tutto won the Tylenol/Arthritis Foundation design award because the weight of the bag is carried on four wheels so pulling is easier.

- More wheels! Four wheels that allow a bag to swivel 360° are now available. Four wheels easily roll through airplane aisles and crowded airports, don't tip over, can be pulled or pushed, and can carry more weight than a two-wheeled bag. But a four-wheeled bag can roll around on its own, whereas a two-wheeled bag stays where it it placed.

- Carry-on luggage is more restricted. Transportation Security Administration (TSA) regulations limit passengers on domestic flights to one carry-on bag not to exceed 45 linear inches (length + width + depth — see page 99), plus one personal item such as a purse, laptop, or briefcase. This has created multi-function, wheeled bags that are a briefcase, laptop carrier, and an overnight bag all in one.

Interesting innovations such as "SkyRoll®" and "SkyRoll® on Wheels" make carry-on even easier. A lightweight garment bag wraps around a core holding shoes and toiletries to create an easy-to-carry or roll-aboard bag that minimizes wrinkling. (See Resources page 239.)

- Manufacturers added expansion gussets to carry-on bags that expand space by as much as 3". When in use, however, the bag will not fit into an airline overhead bin. Use the gusset — check the bag!

- Passengers are checking bags more often, creating an increase in sales of hard-sided luggage that withstands abuse.

- Color is returning to luggage. From lime green to more subtle copper, basic black is getting competition. Color makes locating the right bag at the airport easier, but travel is dirty business and lighter colors show soil more quickly.

Build Your Luggage Wardrobe

It's a good idea to work toward having a luggage wardrobe so that you can choose the right bag for each trip. Review "Match Your Luggage to Your Travel Style" on page 80. This is you and how you travel today. Just because you hope to take an adventure trip "someday" doesn't mean that you need to own luggage for that trip today. Knowing the type of traveler you are will help you determine the best bags for your needs.

Susan's LUGGAGE WARDROBE

LUGGAGE	USE
• Zip-top nylon tote	Great for weekends and tucking into a suitcase as an expansion bag
• Zippered carry-on (3-zip type)	Car trips; too old and fragile for other travel
• Slightly structured small duffel	Once a perfect carry-on but now for car trips because it has no wheels
• Slightly structured garment bag	Same as duffel, above
• 28" hard-sided, wheeled bag	Perfect for "Princess-style" international trips (when I don't have to lift it)
• 26" wheeled, semi-soft, vertical Pullman	May replace 28" bag, above, for long domestic and international trips; I can lift it.
• 22" wheel-aboard	My most used piece for all shorter air-travel trips and when packing light is essential
• Rolling carry-on tote bag	Holds in-flight necessities; piggybacks onto either a 22"or 26"wheel-aboard for easy rolling.

I am prepared for any kind of travel because I've built a luggage wardrobe that matches my travel styles. In my luggage closet you will find the pieces shown in the chart to the left.

With these eight pieces, I have luggage that meets all my needs and I use every piece — just not all on the same trip! If I were selecting new luggage today, I might not purchase these pieces, but they're what I have now and I can tailor them to fit my travel style. I don't toss out old favorites when I buy new pieces. Instead, I relegate my older bags to car trips where wheels and high-tech features are less important.

Decide how you can use the luggage you already own that is in good condition or pass it on to someone who can. Then plan what you need to add to make your luggage wardrobe serve you well.

Today's Luggage Types

The chart on the next pages describes the five basic types of luggage available today, along with advantages and disadvantages for each. In the "Choose For" column you will see the best bag for different styles of trips. "Companion Pieces" are bags that work well together should you need more packing space. Generally, two smaller bags are more manageable than expanding to one larger bag.

Buy the Best Bag for You

There are at least two formal resources you can read when you get ready to purchase new luggage as well as some less formal ways for conducting research. *Consumer Reports* magazine regularly writes about luggage. They test bags in a category and come up with detailed ratings. Even if you don't purchase one of the bags from the test, you will learn the key characteristics that *Consumer Reports* uses to rate luggage.

The Travel Goods Association (TGA) has a website (see "Resources," page 240). "How to Select Luggage—a Buyers Guide" is one of the topics they discuss.

Karen says she looks at well-dressed frequent flyers in the airport or hotel and scrutinizes their luggage choices. She often stops them and says, "Please tell me how you like your suitcase; I'm in the market for a new one." She gets interesting feedback directly

(continued on page 88)

TODAY'S LUGGAGE TYPES

	DESCRIPTION	CHOOSE FOR
Pullman 	Rectangular box with a handle on long side. Classic shape is both today's vertical wheel-aboard and Mom's 1935 Hartmann. Some zip along three sides creating one large packing space; others hinge on long side and open in half or 1/3-2/3 to form two divided sections. Available in hard-sided, semi-soft, and soft-sided constructions, with and without wheels.	• Wheel-aboard style great for business travel. • Works well for city, country, and resort trips.
Garment Bag 	Holds clothing on hangers. May have additional interior and exterior pockets, plus a shoulder strap or wheels and pull handle. Some have an exterior hook for hanging without unpacking. Available in semi-soft and soft-sided versions.	• Compact, wheel-aboard style great for business travel. • Soft suit/dress bags good for car travel. • Works well for all but adventure trips.
Zippered Carry-on 	Rectangular bag with a carrying handle and shoulder strap. Has soft frame shaped with padding and edge piping, zippers and thin dividers form one to three compartments. Often sold as companion piece to wheel-aboard. Soft-sided only.	• Businesslike look. • Good where it can be attached to a wheeled bag or used with separate luggage cart. • Works well for city, country and resorts.
Duffel	Soft-sided, frameless, and lightweight. May be one compartment or may have inside and outside dividers and pockets. Available with zippered sections that can expand bag capacity as needed. Sized by cubic inches of capacity. Soft-side only.	• Best choice for bulky gear for sport, resort, or adventure trips where no one cares about wrinkles! • Softness allows squeezing into car trunk or other tight places.
Travel Pack 	Available frameless or with internal or exterior frame (used by serious backpackers and not discussed here). Frameless packs (day packs) have padded shoulder straps with several zippered sections. Internal-frame models (primary luggage) come with padded shoulder straps and hip/waist belt. New combo bags that look like soft-sided Pullmans feature backpack straps that tuck away in a zippered pocket until needed. Wheels and a pull-handle style are also available.	• Great for any casual trip where your luggage must accompany you everywhere. • Perfect for adventure travel.

ADVANTAGES	DISADVANTAGES	COMPANION PIECES
• Easy to pack; many contain special organizing features like a "suiter" – a section with hangers and a padded flap that cushions folds in a suit or a dress; speeds packing and minimizes wrinkles. • Easy to live out of without unpacking. • Best protection of contents when properly packed. • Available in many sizes and with different interior configurations.	• One big compartment allows contents to shift if not carefully packed; best if packed full to prevent wrinkling. • Bulky to store unless several bags nest together.	Add: garment bag, zippered carry-on, travel pack (one piece should have wheels).
• Fast and easy to pack. • Clothing hangs, minimizing wrinkles. • No need to unpack; hang at destination. • The best way to travel with formal evening wear. • Available in many sizes and styles from compact carry-on to huge, and from soft nylon suit/dress bags to structured cases.	• Structured styles are bulky to store. • Many bags are too large to carry on due to new strict rules.	Add: Pullman, zippered carry-on, travel pack (one piece should have wheels).
• Easy to organize contents: clean vs. dirty, warm vs. cool, casual vs. dressy clothing. • Divided sections keep contents in place, minimizing wrinkling even when not packed tightly. • Flexible so can be expanded or squeezed into smaller spaces. • Stores flat, saving space.	• No wheels so a luggage cart may be required if this is your only bag and it is heavy.	Add: Pullman on wheels, garment bag on wheels, travel pack on wheels.
• Lighter weight and less expensive than more structured bags. • Stores flat to save space. • Flexible, especially expansion sections. • Ideal for sailing trips with minimal storage. • Excellent for packing bulky sports clothing: ski wear or sports gear (wet suits or waders). • Available in a wide range of sizes.	• Little protection of contents so best used for casual clothing that can be rolled or stuffed.	Add: Pullman on wheels; garment bag on wheels; travel pack on wheels.
• Allows hands-free travel and freedom to move without lugging luggage. • Many are expandable and come with a removable day pack. • Wheeled backpacks offer great flexibility; wheels for smooth surfaces and backpacking capability for uneven terrain.	• Little protection of contents so best used for casual wear that can be rolled or stuffed. • Bags often very casual in design and do not have a businesslike appearance.	Add: Duffel (one of the pieces should have wheels).

(continued from page 85)

from the user. I have always learned a lot by going to my local luggage store and asking questions. My favorite person is Fred, the luggage repairman (and salesman supreme); he knows all about durability. When pressed, he will dish out the dirt about which luggage comes back again and again for repairs and which luggage hardly ever returns once sold.

Fred asks the following questions to decide which luggage is best for the customer:

1. **How much do you travel?**
   This determines potential use; frequent flyers require more durability than the occasional traveler.

2. **On average, how long will you be gone on a trip?**
   This determines the size of the bag or the number of pieces needed.

Pull handle should telescope, feel comfortable in hand, fit your height.

Look for These Features

Vertical Pullman Wheel-aboard

hooks or piggyback straps to hold extra bags

pockets you can use

carrying handle on top and side

expandable gussets to add up to 3" of packing space

durable fabric

zippers — bigger is better

corner shields and stair climber skids to protect fabric

bottom handle to make lifting easier

large pull tabs with a hole for sturdy lock

wheels — ball-bearing type is best

With answers to these questions, he can best advise a customer about the details that count: warranty; fabric; wheels; handles; and zippers.

Warranty: Most warranties cover manufacturing defects only. The warranties vary from nothing to 10 years to a lifetime and all but one exclude airline damage — Briggs and Riley. They say "Our warranty covers taxi driver damage, under-tipped bellhop damage, rabid dog damage, dragged-five-miles-behind-a-bus damage, even airline damage. Simple as that.^{sm}" Fred says that Briggs and Riley bags come back for very simple repairs. Even though they have the best warranty, often it isn't necessary because Briggs and Riley bags are so well built.

Fabric: Judged by thickness of fiber or "denier," the higher the denier the stronger the fabric.

- **Nylon** is one of the most popular luggage coverings. Look for 1,000+ denier or 11-ounce nylon for durability. "Ballistic" nylon is similar to the fabric used in bulletproof vests. In luggage, it resists tearing better than other fabrics. Cordura® (developed by DuPont for automobile tires so it is strong!) and Cordura Plus® are high quality, abrasion-and-tear-resistant nylons.

  Look for waterproof coatings that are applied to the inside and soil-resistant coatings to the outside. Scotchgard®, Zepel®, and Teflon® are some names to look for on a label.

- **Polyester** does not resist abrasion as well as nylon so a higher denier is very important. Look for at least 1,000 denier polyester. Polyester appears most frequently in lower to mid-priced luggage and is fine for the occasional traveler.

- **Vinyl** is used more for piping and trims than for a full bag covering because it tends to tear. It is also used as a backing for nylon fabrics to add body and make them more water-resistant.

- **Plastics** are used to make injection-molded, hard-sided luggage. They are durable, waterproof, and stain resistant.

- **Leather** is an elegant, expensive, and heavy luggage covering. It is still available in high-end bags but is most often used today for piping, trims, and straps.

Wheels: Ball-bearing wheels (the type used on in-line skates) are best and should be partially recessed for protection. Most new bags have two wheels and a pull handle; those with four wheels are thought to put less strain on the pulling arm. Be sure to test in the store for maneuverability. Load the bag with some heavy store merchandise (pulling it empty will not tell what you need to know) and pull it around. Go over bumps and on and off the carpet, simulating the movements you will make while traveling with the bag. Look for substantial stair-climber skids — plastic shields that make it easier to pull a bag up stairs and curbs without damaging the fabric. Test the bag on stairs too.

Susan's LUGGAGE SHOPPING TIPS

1. Before you shop, be clear about your needs. I recently shopped for a new bag (my new 26" wheeled vertical Pullman was the result) and found it confusing. The following points helped me make my decision:

·   Know exactly what you want the bag to do and how much you are willing to spend. "I need a large, lightweight bag with wheels to replace my 28" hard-sided bag, especially for international travel. My price range is $____ to $_____."

·   Know the size you need. Bags are measured in two ways: by length measurement (my 26" bag), and by volume stated in cubic inches. I found the volume measurement to be the most accurate and easiest to compare, as one maker's 26" bag was very different from another. To find the volume, multiply length times width times depth and compare. My new bag is smaller in length but deeper so the volume is actually greater than my old one.

length x width x depth = volume in cubic inches

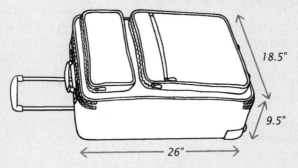

old bag: 28" x 20" x 7.5" = 4200 cubic inches
new bag: 26" x 18.5" x 9.5" = 4569 cubic inches

Handles and straps: Pull-handles should be the right length for your height for comfortable use and should lock in the extended and stowed-away positions. Handles should feel comfortable in your hand. A bag should have carry handles on the side and top for carrying and when lifting it into storage compartments. Look for removable shoulder straps that can be tucked into a carry-on when checking. Padding on the strap is also essential for comfort.

2. **Learn to recognize quality merchandise.** I recommend shopping at different types of stores: luggage and travel stores (usually the most informed retailers), mass merchandisers, discount stores, wholesale clubs, and department stores all sell luggage. You will see many different qualities and price ranges and only you will know which one meets your travel needs and is within your budget. After you have shopped in person you will be knowledgeable enough to shop from a mail-order catalog or on-line. I waited for a sale at my local luggage store and was happy with the guidance I received from my salesperson. The bag I purchased and the price were just right for me.

3. **Give it the "pack test."** Pack it to see if it will hold what you want to take before you actually use it. You can decide whether to keep the bag or take it back. This was super advice from my salesperson. Once I packed my bag I was sold. Use this opportunity to test pulling a packed bag on different terrain.

4. **Choose inconspicuous luggage.** This is not a place to display your love of luxury goods. A really expensive bag shouts "Steal Me First! I am filled with great stuff!" Some use this to advantage, traveling with their most valuable things in dumpy old bags. Who would know?

5. **Dark colors show dirt the least.** There is a reason most luggage is available in black. To distinguish your black bag from others, mark it in a visible way (see page 97 for ideas).

6. **Make sure the bag is comfortable for you.** Airports are large and we often must pull our bags for long distances so bags should feel good. Is the handle the right length? I own a bag that was built for a six-footer and I am 5'3". Does the handle feel good in your hand? One of my bag handles has ridges that hurt my hands when I pull the fully packed bag for any distance.

Zippers and locks: The zipper is frequently the item that fails on luggage. Bigger is better as size indicates strength. The main zipper should be at least a #6. Zippers wear better if they are placed away from the edge. They should have a pull tab large enough to hold onto comfortably and the pull tab should have a hole for a lock. Sturdy combination locks are more secure than little key locks. Since every hotel bell desk has a set of standard luggage keys, a combination lock is the safest bet. It's smart to know the combination to your traveling companion's bag too.

SMART TRAVEL

Grant suggests using a twist tie as an emergency lock. It won't keep the truly determined out of your bag but will prevent the casual thief with little time from gaining access to your things.

SMART TRAVEL *Security Update*

The TSA advises that all airline checked baggage must be unlocked for possible manual checking. If your bag has been x-rayed and needs further inspection, a TSA screener will open your bag and check the contents. The screener will leave a note or sticker stating that they have opened your bag. They may also attach a tamper-proof plastic "lock" after inspection.

Don't forget to take locks with you so you can secure your bag after leaving the airport. It's always wise to lock your bags when they are in the car and in your hotel room.

SMART TRAVEL *Gadget*

TSA-approved locks now allow for securing checked bags. Available in both combination and key versions, these sturdy locks keep out thieves yet allow security screeners access with a universal key. See www.travelsentry.org or www.safeskieslocks.com.

CHAPTER 10

Checking or Carrying Bags?

Consider the contingencies and factor in fatigue. Today's travel gets more complicated by the minute. What if you had to hustle for a tight connection — could you make it with your carry-on bags?

Check it or carry it on board — that is the question on many travelers' minds as they choose what to take and which luggage to use. Business travelers on tight schedules may have a different view of the subject than leisure travelers.

I'm stating my opinion here: I prefer to check my bags for everything beyond an overnight or very short trip. I plan my trips to allow enough time for checking my luggage and claiming it at the other end. I don't *want* to drag my wheel-aboard along miles of airport concourses; I'm not strong enough or tall enough to lift a loaded bag up into the overhead bin; and I *do* have faith that my checked luggage *will be there* when I want to claim it.

I spent my working career traveling with two large checked bags and my carry-on was a heavy slide projector. I never lost a bag. Yes, my bags have been delayed but not often so I don't fear checking my bags.

I now see virtue in traveling lighter, but lighter does not have to mean carry-on. My packing list on page 22 reflects needing to travel light by train and car; on international flights I check my bag. Checking baggage works for me and it may work for you too.

Know the TSA Checked Baggage Rules

New security measures are in place for all types of transportation. Airlines, trains, and buses now require higher levels of security, with airlines being the most specific. For current airline security information, check www.smartpacking.com or www.tsa.dot.gov. Follow these rules and your bags will easily pass security.

1. All airline checked baggage is now screened for explosive devices by the TSA using several methods; some are visible in the airport lobby and some out of view in the baggage areas.

2. **Bags must be unlocked** to allow for possible manual checking of contents. TSA-approved locks are an exception and may be used (see page 92).

3. You must check your bags yourself and show current government-issued photo identification (driver's license or passport). Be prepared to present your photo ID and boarding pass at the airline check-in counter, at the security checkpoint, and again at the gate. There may be additional screening at the gate.

4. No sharp objects of any kind or size are allowed into an aircraft cabin; they will be confiscated by airport security. Pocket-knives, sharp-pointed scissors, corkscrews, and multi-purpose tools may be packed in checked baggage, but not in carry-on.

Pack Checked Bags for Easy Screening

1. **Do not pack food in checked bags.** Chocolate, cheese, and other foods have the same density as explosives and may trigger a manual bag search. Carry these items in your carry-on bag instead.

2. **Avoid stacking dense items** such as books — spread them out in a single layer for easier viewing.

3. **Group small items in clear see-through containers** or plastic bags to make the contents of your bag easy for security screeners to check and repack.

4. **Pack less or take two lightly packed bags** instead of one that is too full. Over-filled bags take longer to check manually and are more difficult for security screeners to repack, with the possibility that your luggage could miss your flight.

5. **Place shoes on top** as they may contain metal parts that require hand inspection. Use clear shoe bags, not cloth ones.

Follow Airline Bag Size and Weight Rules

Domestic airlines have begun diligently enforcing bag size and weight regulations that have been in existence for some time. They are now charging hefty fees for overweight bags, oversized bags, and for checking more than the two bags allowed per passenger. Rules differ from one airline to another so it is important to check by phone or on the website before traveling. International rules vary by destination so be sure to check with your airline.

Domestic Airline Baggage Limitations

1. **You are allowed two checked bags per ticketed passenger.** Extra bags will be accepted for a fee. In addition, each passenger may carry on one bag not exceeding 45 linear inches, and one small personal item such as a purse or briefcase. Exception: Some discount airlines are now charging fees for all checked bags. Check with your airline to know their policy.

2. **Your largest checked bag may not exceed 62 linear inches (length + width + depth).** Oversized bags are accepted for a fee.

3. **No bag may weigh more than 50 pounds on many airlines.** (Call your carrier to verify.) Fees are charged on bags weighing between 50 and 70 pounds, and higher fees for bags weighing over 70 pounds. Airlines will not accept bags weighing over 100 pounds — these must be shipped as cargo.

The Fees are High!

If you think you will simply pay the fee, here is an example of what overpacking can cost.

Excess bag fee:	$80	(per bag over the two bags allowed)
Oversized bag fee:	$100	(measures more than 62 linear inches)
Overweight bag fee:	$50	(weighs between 50 and 70 pounds)
	or$100	(weighs between 70 and 100 pounds)
TOTAL:	at least $230	total excess baggage fees **for one way!**

Fees are charged on a one-way basis — double this figure if you are traveling round trip. Also, fees vary by destination. Some commuter airlines may not accept any excess, oversized or overweight bags. Don't forget that for most travelers, luggage gets heavier as the trip progresses!

There Are Exceptions

Each airline has a different ruling on kid's gear (child safety seat, umbrella stroller), sports equipment (for golfing, fishing, or skiing), military bags, or mobility devices. **Call or visit your airline's website to check in advance so you are not surprised at the airport.**

The Solution: Plan Ahead

1. **Know the size of your bag.** Before you begin packing, measure your bag to determine its linear dimensions. Be sure to include the handle and wheels in this measurement. See page 99 for exactly how to measure.

2. **Decide now to pack into two smaller bags that will be easier to lift and maneuver** as you travel, rather than use one oversized bag. Often two smaller bags will fit into a car, guest room, or hotel room more easily than one very large bag.

3. **Weigh each packed bag on your bathroom scale before leaving for the airport.** You'll know right away if your bag is over 50 pounds while you still have time to remove heavy items and leave them at home. Imagine how difficult this will be at the airport check-in counter! I recently watched as a couple frantically moved items from bag to bag to distribute weight, displaying various unmentionables to those waiting in line. They managed to move enough to not pay a fee, but missed their flight in the process.

4. **Review "Nine Ways to Pack Less" on page 23** for easy ways to travel lighter.

SMART TRAVEL *Security Update*

Kodak recommends not packing unprocessed film or single-use cameras in checked luggage, as higher doses of radiation are being used on checked baggage than in the past. Film becomes fogged when exposed to high-intensity, x-ray exposure; lead-lined bags no longer offer adequate protection. Here are some suggestions for traveling with film:

1. Buy and process film at your destination.

2. Carry film with you and politely request a hand inspection of high-speed specialty film (ASA/ISO of 800 or higher). The TSA suggests carrying film in clear canisters or a clear plastic bag for easier screening.

3. Don't worry about sending your lower ASA film from your vacation through x-ray screening in your carry-on bag — unless your film will be screened more than five times.

4. Purchase a digital camera. There is no film so no damage can be done.

The Ten Best Baggage-Checking Habits

1. **Adhere to the rules.**
   Know the baggage limits for each leg of your trip so you can pack smart. On most domestic flights, two checked bags are allowed per ticketed passenger. (See previous pages for details). On some international segments, baggage allowances are determined by weight rather than by number of pieces so know the rules before packing.

2. **Use sturdy ID tags.**
   Always have an ID tag on every bag, carry-ons included. Use a sturdy tag with a durable strap—airline paper tags with elastic straps are a very poor, emergency-only choice. The best tags have a cover hiding your name. This cover could be a photo of you — proof of ownership in any language. To protect your privacy, use your business address and phone whenever possible.

3. **Include your identification information inside the bag.**
   This is especially important if the outside tag is lost en route. Place an itinerary in an outside pocket or inside your bag on top so the airline can track you in transit, in the event your bag is delayed or misrouted.

4. **Check your bags as early as possible.**
   Airlines suggest at least 90 minutes in advance (two hours for international travel) but at daily high-traffic times and with seasonal crowding you should add 30 minutes to this time. Last-minute checked bags simply may not make it through security screening to the plane, so check in early. I enjoy having a relaxed snack before a flight or having time to place phone calls so always check in early. You can use any extra time before boarding to shop, have breakfast, or read the paper.

5. **Remove any old baggage claim tags from your luggage.**
   They can cause destination confusion. Take off any detachable straps and tuck them into your carry-on bag. Loose straps get caught in the baggage-handling systems and can seriously damage your bag as well as the machinery.

6. **Mark your bags well.**
   Mark clearly so you can recognize your black bag in a sea of black bags. Distinctive marks emphasize ownership quickly. Put a big X on each side with colored tape; attach a bright ribbon tightly to the handle; put your initials in large, colored, stick-on letters on the sides; or apply unique bright stickers.

For added security, use a brightly colored strap around the middle of the bag to hold it together in case of zipper or latch failure — this makes your bag easier to identify too.

SMART TRAVEL *Gadget*

Brightly colored nylon or neoprene grips that wrap around the handle of a bag with Velcro® make your bag easy to locate. Check your favorite luggage or travel store.

7. **Make sure that your bags have been ticketed to the correct destination and on the correct flight numbers before you leave the sky cap area or ticket counter.**
   Airlines now tag bags with bar codes, which is much more accurate than the old visual system, but it is still possible for an error to occur. Barbara W.'s bags were checked to the wrong Portland on a business trip, but she knew the airport codes and caught the error before it was too late.

8. **Do a bag count every time you check or claim bags.**
   Do it when you board or exit a bus or taxi, or arrive at or depart from a hotel, too.

9. **Insure your bags (if this important to you).**
   Ask for "excess valuation" at the ticket counter. Your bags will be tagged with a code that lets baggage handlers know that these bags get special treatment and extra careful routing. This increases the airline's liability to as high as $5,000 at a cost of about $2 to $5 per $100 (cost varies between airlines). Under current rules, airlines are liable for only up to $3000 for baggage loss or damage. See page 103 for more on insurance.

10. **Always pack a survival kit in your carry-on.**
    Include basics needed should your bags be delayed. I pack a small cosmetics case, prescriptions and other medications, a change of underwear, and a clean blouse.

Know the Carry-on Baggage Rules

Follow these TSA carry-on luggage rules now in effect in every airport to ensure a stress-free trip.

1. **One carry-on bag per passenger on domestic flights, plus one personal item. The bag may not exceed 45 linear inches (length + width + depth). Personal items can be a purse, laptop, briefcase, or bag that will fit under the seat in front of you.**

   Pack your carry-on bag so the contents are easily examined. See-through containers speed hand checking of cosmetics or groups of clothing. International carriers may be more restrictive so contact each carrier you will be traveling on and ask about their carry-on policies.

2. **No knives or cutting instruments of any size allowed in an aircraft cabin, train, or bus.** Pocketknives may be carried only in checked baggage. No sharp object of any kind or size is allowed to pass through security checkpoints on your person or in a carry-on bag. Pack these items in checked baggage only.

3. **Measure your carry-on, wheel-aboard bag carefully.** The maximum allowable total dimension is 45 linear inches. Length + width + depth = linear inches; be sure to include wheels and handle. Measure the bag yourself; do not simply read the dimensions on a tag. Often the manufacturer measures the packable *interior* size of the bag, not the exterior (including wheels and handle). If you pack in the exterior pockets, your bag may be rejected by the airline "sizer box," so be sure to allow for an expanded size when measuring.

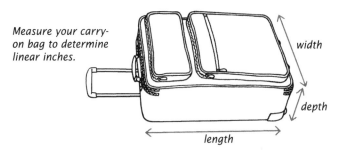

Measure your carry-on bag to determine linear inches.

width

depth

length

length + width + depth = linear inches

4. **Investigate purchasing a carry-on that is even smaller than 45 linear inches.** This strategy allows for using the exterior pockets and an expandable gusset and still passing the "sizer box" test. The question is, can you cut back more and pack less in this smaller space?

5. **Always be prepared to check your bag** since the rules can change in the middle of your trip. Plan to put anything you will need during the flight in a "too-small-to-question" tote bag or briefcase along with any valuables. See the list of items to always have in your possession below.

6. **Don't plan to hang anything** in the aircraft closet as these no longer exist in many airplanes.

7. **Make sure carry-on pieces have substantial identification tags** (not the flimsy paper tags airlines issue), especially those that might have to be checked at the gate if required by the airline at the last minute. Label your bags on the inside too.

Carry These With You

If you are asked to check your bag because of the new carry-on restrictions, insist on taking a minute to go through the bag and remove any valuable or irreplaceable items. Place them in your "too-small-to-question" tote bag or briefcase. These items are always safer in your possession:

address book	eyeglasses
business papers	jewelry
camcorders	keys
cameras/exposed film	medications/prescriptions
cash and credit cards	passport
CD/DVD/MP3 player	personal computer/pda
cellular phones	toiletries/cosmetics kit
change of underwear	travel documents

SMART TRAVEL

Barbara A. recommends carrying on anything that, if lost, will ruin your trip (ski boots), expensive necessities (eyeglasses), and anything irreplaceable (tax records, family heirlooms).

CARRY-ON COURTESY

If you decide to carry your bags on board, there are rules of etiquette that you should honor so you, your fellow travelers, and airline personnel will be comfortable and worry-free while on board. Consider these guidelines:

· It is your job to lift your carry-on bag into the overhead bin. This is not the responsibility of the flight attendant or a kindly fellow passenger. If you can't lift it, you should check it.

· The seats with the largest under-seat area are usually the much despised center seats. The window seat storage is limited by the curvature of the aircraft and the aisle seat storage by a seat post. If you must put your bag under the seat in front of you, the center seat is the best choice. If that's not your assigned seat, don't assume that you can use it until you check with your seat-mate. However, even this space may not hold a 22" wheel-aboard bag.

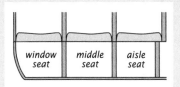

· As the airlines reconfigure aircraft to hold more passengers, the seats not only get narrower but the rows become closer together, creating less leg room. If you were able to get your wheel-aboard under the seat in the past, you probably will not be able to do so now. There simply is not enough room between your seat and the back of the seat in front of you to squeeze your bag underneath. The overhead bin is your best bet. One of Barbara W.'s pet peeves is the passenger who insists on trying to muscle a bag into a too-small space, holding up the boarding process as a result!

· Boarding the aircraft as soon as you are allowed to do so (when your row or travel status is called) is essential for finding space for your carry-on items. He who hesitates has his bag checked at the gate.

· Avoid placing your bag in an overhead bin behind you if at all possible. You will have to go against traffic to retrieve it before deplaning, another very unpopular move.

Managing Delayed or Lost Baggage

Baggage is delayed more frequently than it is lost — and usually arrives on the very next flight. In fact, 98% of delayed bags are returned to their owners within hours. This is a small consolation if your baggage misses the connection to your international flight or to your cruise. When Pati's luggage found it's way to Japan for a month while she was en route to six different US cities, she discovered that she could live quite well with the few things she had in her carry-on. It changed her personal travel packing forever.

To prevent your bags from straying off the planned route, it is essential to develop good bag-checking habits. Review the "Ten Best Baggage Checking Habits" on pages 97-98.

Six Steps to Recover Lost Bags

If your bags do go astray, follow these important steps to ensure a speedy reunion.

1. **Report missing bags immediately to the airline service desk,** usually located in the baggage claim area. *Do not leave the airport and think you will do this later.* The sooner your bag is noted as "lost in the system" the sooner it will be located and returned to you.

2. **Fill out a loss report form.** You will need your baggage claim tag. Bar code tags for routing baggage make the search and recovery process easier than in the past, but if the tag comes off, you must be able to describe your bags as accurately as possible. Include a photo of your luggage in the travel documents that you carry at all times or on your cell phone or digital camera. Many people try to report a lost bag but don't remember the size, brand, shape, or color.

3. **Be sure to ask for a copy of any form you sign with the date and time of filing in writing.** Write down the name, title, and telephone number of any airline employee you deal with and get a toll-free number for tracking the progress of your bag.

4. **Do not give the airline your baggage claim tag unless they provide a photocopy.** It's your only hard evidence that you checked that bag.

5. **Provide the airline with the address of where you are stay-ing or your forward itinerary** so they can deliver the delayed

luggage to you. Don't assume the airline will deliver the bag to you without charge when it is found; ask about this when you file your lost bag claim.

6. **Ask for authorization to purchase necessities** if the airline cannot track your bag to know when it will arrive and you face an overnight without your things. They will not offer you anything beyond a free kit of supplies, but when pressed may agree to reimburse you for some basics. Save all receipts. If your bags are delayed a day or more, ask for authorization for additional purchases. If the airline misplaces sporting equipment, it will sometimes pay for the rental of replacements.

What About Forever Lost or Damaged Bags?

Airlines are liable for damage or loss of your checked or carry-on baggage up to a maximum of $3000 per person on domestic flights. On international flights the limit is set by treaty at $20 per kilogram (about $9 per pound) of checked baggage weight. The airline is liable for depreciated value, not replacement value or original purchase price. **That's not very much.**

1. **Check your homeowner's or renter's policy to see if it covers your personal effects while traveling** in order to cover the difference between what an airline is responsible for and the value of the contents. Some charge cards (at gold or platinum levels) include baggage insurance. You can also investigate an annual personal property policy. "Excess valuation insurance" (see page 98) purchased from the airline at the check-in counter is another option.

2. **Keep a copy of your packing list at home** so you know what was in the lost or damaged bag. Most travelers can't remember all the contents of a suitcase, particularly when they have more than one. To validate your claim, you must know exactly what was lost or damaged.

SMART TRAVEL TIP

The *Wall Street Journal* reported that if your bag is damaged by airline baggage handlers you should ask the airline for a new one. Some carriers actually keep a few extra suitcases just in case yours comes off the carousel and is completely unusable. This saves you from having to check into your hotel with your belongings in a plastic trash bag — not a pretty sight!

CHAPTER 11

Packing Like a Pro

If you think packing is a pain, join the club!

Some people just hate to pack, considering it the worst part of the trip. I should know — I'm married to one such reluctant packer. David complains, procrastinates, threatens to stay home, and begs me to help (translate that to: do it all). I packed his bags when he was the harried traveling executive, but another person can't do it all. He is the only one who can make the decisions about which items work best for his trip. So, there comes the time when you must buck up and start packing your own bags! Take my ideas and tailor them to fit your travel plans.

Assemble Your Packing Tools

Before packing, you'll want several tools to make the job easier. Following are items I assemble in Packing Central (see page 43) to keep things organized, clean, and wrinkle-free.

1. **Self-sealing plastic bags in several sizes:** I use two-gallon, one-gallon, quart, and pint sizes for grouping items so they won't get lost. This is a great way to keep categories of things together in one place — a bag for socks, a bag for underwear, etc. Sheila uses zippered mesh laundry bags in various sizes to hold tee-shirts and underwear.

SMART TRAVEL *Security Update*

See-through containers (clear plastic or mesh) make security checks go faster as screeners can easily view the contents without opening each bag.

2. **Plastic dry cleaner's bags:** These protect your clothing and prevent wrinkles by trapping air between layers. I once bought a roll of at least one million from my dry cleaner and am still using them. You can also save the ones that come from the cleaners. Some say the ink on printed plastic bags may come off on clothing but I have never had that problem. If this worries you, turn the bags inside out.

3. **Tissue paper:** I don't use much, but it does come in handy for stuffing the sleeves of a delicate jacket, for instance.

4. **Clothes dryer softener sheets:** Tuck one into your suitcase to keep the contents sweet smelling. You can also use it in the dryer at the self-service laundry.

5. **Bags for shoes:** I prefer clear plastic bags from the grocery produce department so I can see the shoe inside. Other choices are old socks or purchased shoe bags. One shoe per bag allows for more flexible packing. Susan H. uses a clear plastic hotel shower cap for each shoe.

SMART TRAVEL *Security Update*

The TSA recommends packing shoes last, on top of other contents. Shoes often contain metal parts that make it necessary to do a hand inspection of your bag; packing shoes on top speeds the process.

6. **Vacuum cleaner:** Use the edge-cleaner tool to vacuum the lint and sand from the last trip out of the bottom of the suitcase.

7. **Solid-color bed sheet:** Place a clean sheet on top of the bedspread so road dirt and dust on the suitcase won't soil the spread. The solid-color helps me find small items that may get lost in the design of my printed bedspread.

8. **Nylon zip-top tote:** Select a bag that fits in the bottom of your main suitcase to be used as an "overflow bag" for shipping home dirty laundry or accumulated treasures.

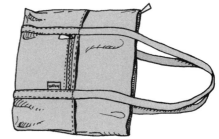

9. **Bubble wrap:** Packing a bag completely full minimizes shifting of contents and wrinkling. Items shift toward the bottom, which can change depending on how the bag is carried or rolled. If your bag is not quite full, add sheets of bubble wrap. Toss the bubble wrap as you add purchases and the contents expand. Or, keep the bubble wrap to use for packing fragile items you find along the way.

SMART TRAVEL *Gadget*

Look for Pack-It® Folders, Pack-It Cubes, and Pack-It Sacs by Eagle Creek (www.eaglecreek.com) in luggage and travel stores or catalogs. These handy organizers are a step up from my plastic bags! Similar products from other makers are also available.

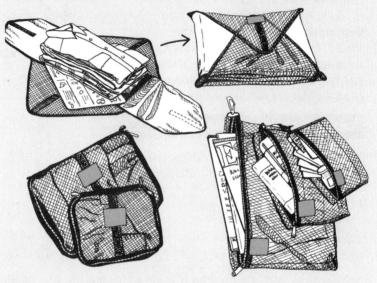

Compression bags are reusable plastic bags that reduce the volume of clothing by up to 75%. They have a unique, one-way valve that allows the air to be compressed out of the bag, leaving a much flatter bundle. They work best with casual clothing or dirty laundry where wrinkling is not an issue, or use them to pack your favorite down pillow. Look for Pack-It® compressor bags (www.eaglecreek.com) or Pack-Mates™ (www.packmate.com) at luggage and travel stores.

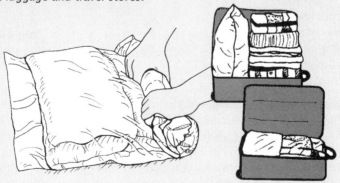

Schedule Your Packing Time

Feeling exhausted and grouchy is no way to begin your trip. Give yourself the gift of extra time to get all those unexpected last-minute things done.

Two days before your departure, **assemble everything you want to pack** in "Packing Central" (see page 43). If you've planned for your trip following the advice in Section I of this book, you have already selected items and "scarecrowed" them (see pages 44-45) into mix-and-match outfits.

Now, start packing. If you find things don't fit, you still have time to edit your choices or switch to different bags. Save the last day before departure for watering the plants and organizing your travel documents and carry-on items.

This is also a good time to test the weight of your packed suitcase. Take it around the block twice, which is about the distance from the average airport gate to the parking lot. If this is to be a carry-on bag, see if you can you lift it over your head to place it in the aircraft overhead bin. If not, now is the time to lighten the load; it will only get heavier as you travel. An old Spanish proverb states, "On a long journey, even a piece of straw weighs heavy."

Pack Smart!

Now you're ready to fill your bag. There is a unique way to pack in each luggage type to travel most efficiently. Packing a garment bag requires a different method than packing a duffel, so read the following basic information and then go to the specifics for your type of bag. Here are three universal packing techniques that apply to many of the luggage types:

1. **Grouping** is simply placing similar small items in a container to keep them together so you won't have to search the entire bag to find what you need.

If you are staying in a different hotel every night, grouping makes packing and unpacking much faster and easier for quick in and out. Pack one group of tee-shirts instead of five individual shirts and spend one-fifth the time. For grouping aids, see "Smart Travel Gadgets" on page 106.

SMART TRAVEL

If you're using self-sealing bags for packing, squeeze out the air to make them flatter before zipping.

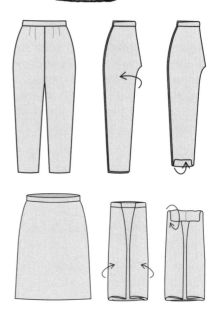

2. **Rolling** works best for casual clothing and packing into a duffel or travel pack. You can then group your rolled tee-shirts into a self-sealing bag or Pack-It Cube. The world is sharply divided between "rollers and folders" and I am a folder. I share rolling with you because half of my survey respondents insist rolling is the gospel of packing. Test and decide for yourself.

To roll pants or a skirt: Fold the pants in half lengthwise and roll from the hem to the waist. Fold a skirt in thirds and roll from waist to hem.

SMART TRAVEL

Tuck a fabric softener dryer sheet inside garments that develop static cling. If you must roll items that wrinkle, place them on a plastic cleaner's bag and then roll, bag and all.

To roll a tee-shirt: Place the shirt face down on a smooth surface and fold in the sleeves. Roll from the hem to the neck, smoothing to remove wrinkles as you roll.

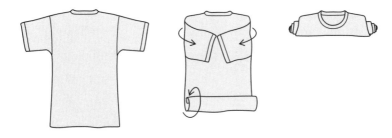

Sheila rolls several items together for speed and organization. Stack several tee-shirts and roll as a unit, or roll tee-shirt, shorts and underwear (a day's outfit) together.

3. **Interfolding** is a method of alternating layers of clothing so they will cushion each other in the suitcase. I've found it to be the most wrinkle-resistant way to pack.

   - Place your longest items in the bag first. Place pants with the waistband against a short end of the suit-case and the legs draped over the oppo-site edge. Top this with a plastic cleaner's bag.

   - Position the next pair of pants with the waistband touching the opposite short end of the suitcase and cover with another cleaner's bag.

   plastic cleaner's bag

• Position a dress with the neck touching the suitcase short end and the skirt draped over the other edge; add a cleaner's bag.

• Place shorter items (jackets, shirts or skirts) with the tops at the hinged or flapped edge and draping over the handle side; add a cleaner's bag.

In a large bag some shorter items may actually fit flat (no folds at all) when placed with the top of the garment at the edge of the bag, and the body parallel to the hinged/flapped edge.

• When all pieces are positioned as described above, with tops alternating, fill in the center with folded dress shirts, folded or rolled tee-shirts, shorts, sweaters, and grouped items in containers. These will help cushion the folds.

• Next, fold in the draped and overlapped edges, smoothing as you go. Interfolding creates a soft roll instead of a flat fold in your clothes.

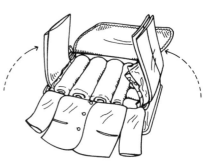

- You may use interfolding with garments on hangers. With one garment on a hanger, cover each with a plastic cleaner's bag. Place one at a time in the suitcase, alternating tops as above. Fold in the draped and overlapped edges.

SMART TRAVEL Tip

An even faster way to interfold is to accordion fold all the individually bagged things on hangers into the suitcase in one group — not as wrinkle-free, but certainly fast and easy to unpack.

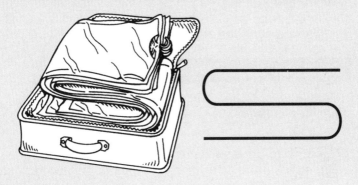

SMART TRAVEL Tip

If you are packing two days early and are worried about wrinkles, interfold as above to verify that all your choices will fit, then unfold the overlapped pieces leaving them layered in the bag until just before you depart. Refold, close, and go. You can also do this if you don't have time to unpack each night.

TRICKS FOR DIFFERENT BAG TYPES

Packing a One-Section Pullman

(Some wheel-aboards are best packed in this three-layer process.)

1. The bottom layer holds heavy and irregularly shaped items, grouped items, plus soft rolled things.
2. The middle layer contains interfolded clothing.
3. The top layer holds the things you need first.

Bottom Layer

1. Completely fill each shoe with underwear, jewelry, pantyhose, socks. This saves space and shapes your shoes. Place the heaviest items (shoes, toiletries, cosmetics, hair dryer) against the hinged edge for carrying or next to the wheels for rolling. Pack belts around the outer edge.

SMART TRAVEL *Security Update*

Remember: For air travel, the TSA recommends packing shoes last, on top of other contents. See page 94.

2. Fill in with rolled small items (tee-shirts, undershirts, exercise wear, swimsuit) or with items grouped in organizers (underwear, socks). This layer should be as level as possible and weight-balanced for either carrying or rolling.

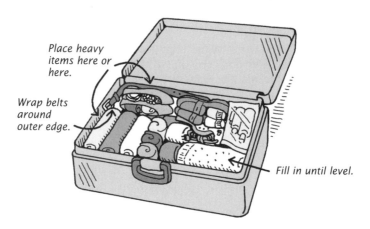

Place heavy items here or here.

Wrap belts around outer edge.

Fill in until level.

Middle Layer

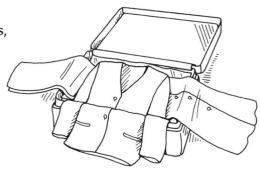

1. This layer is for pants, skirts, jackets, or shirts that you want to fold as few times as possible to prevent wrinkling. Place these in the bag using the interfolding method. Top this layer with a divider (see next page).

2. For instant access to the bottom layer without disturbing the rest of the bag, slide your hands under the divider and gently lift the interfolded clothing out and onto a flat surface. Repeat to repack. This is a quick way to live out of your suitcase without unpacking everything.

3. To remove one item from the interfolded clothing stack, slide your hands on top of the piece you want and gently lift the upper layers out and onto a flat surface. Remove the desired piece, and replace the interfolded layers.

Top Layer

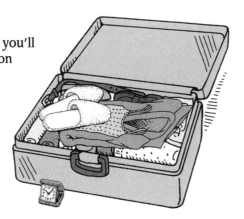

1. Place the first things that you'll need at your destination on top. I put my nightgown, robe, slippers, and clock on top so I can get comfortable first and then unpack. Going to a beach resort? Put your swimsuit, cover-up, and sandals on top.

SMART TRAVEL Tip

Place a plastic cleaner's bag over the bottom layer so you can lift the top two layers up without disturbing anything.

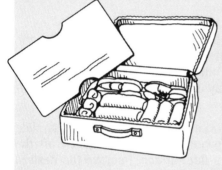

Alternatively, make a divider by cutting a piece of cardboard or poster board to fit the shape of your suitcase, leaving cutouts at the sides for your hands.

June H. uses a paper shopping bag cut along the end folds, then taped together to fit her bag. She lifts up on the handles to raise the top layers.

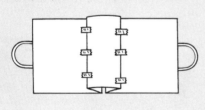

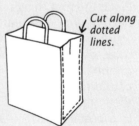

Cut along dotted lines.

Packing a Two-Section Pullman

Two-section Pullmans are usually divided in half or in a 1/3: 2/3 proportion with a shelf or tie-down straps. Some wheel-aboard styles are best packed in this manner, too.

1. Pack the bottom layer as in "Packing a One-Section Pullman" on page 112.

2. Use the top section for your best clothes or for the things that may wrinkle; interfold items to fill that space.

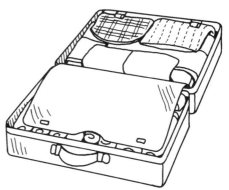

3. Place any remaining items on top of the bottom layer, rolling to fit or folding as few times as possible to minimize wrinkling.

4. Put the first things you will need at your destination on top, as shown on page 113.

SMART TRAVEL *Security Update*

Remember: For air travel, the TSA recommends packing shoes last, on top of other contents. See page 94.

Packing a Garment Bag

The goal in packing a garment bag is to pack several items on each hanger so the clothing cushions itself, along with the help of a few plastic bags.

1. Start with pants. If your garment bag hangers don't have a non-slip crossbar, get some cardboard ones from your dry cleaner. You can also pad this bar with a sweater or tee-shirt. Hang one leg over the crossbar at the knee, then flip the other leg over in the opposite direction as shown. This "locks" the pants over the hanger and prevents them from slipping off.

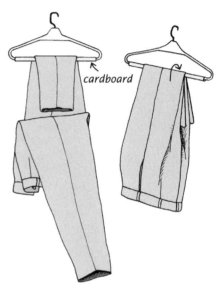

cardboard

2. Hang a shirt or blouse over the pants, buttoning as needed to keep it neatly on the hanger. Hang additional shirts, crossing the sleeves over the chest of the shirt underneath as you button the next one in place. Layer shirts with plastic cleaner's bags if you are afraid they will wrinkle. Hang a jacket over this unit and cover all with a plastic dry cleaner's bag.

Drape a necktie around the jacket neck, hang it over the pants on the crossbar, or roll it up and tuck into a pocket.

SMART TRAVEL TIP

Hang a different outfit on each hanger, perfectly coordinated at home, to eliminate any need to think while dressing each day on the road.

3. Fold skirts over a hanger crossbar and layer with shirts or blouses and jackets as shown for pants. If packing pants and a skirt, start with the pants and add the skirt next. Fold a skirt in thirds, avoiding a center front fold that is the most visible. Hang scarves over the skirt or pant.

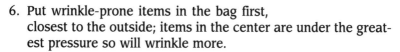

4. Layer dresses over small blouses and under jackets, adding plastic bags to avoid wrinkles if needed.

5. For packing a fragile item such as formal wear for a cruise, place a plastic bag on the hanger first, then the garment, then stuff or pad with tissue paper in the neckline, sleeves, collar, and any other area that may crush; top with another plastic bag.

6. Put wrinkle-prone items in the bag first, closest to the outside; items in the center are under the greatest pressure so will wrinkle more.

7. Fill in around hangers and corners with cosmetics in plastic bags, shoes in protective bags, rolled items, or small items grouped in bags. Fill pockets with grouped underwear, socks, pantyhose.

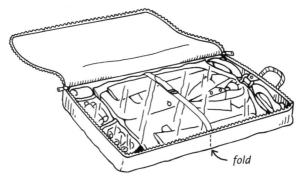

fold

Packing a Zippered Carry-on

These bags are the most difficult to describe because so many variations exist. There are one-, two- or three-zip styles, giving multiple sections to pack. Some have zippers that expand the bag to hold greater volume; some have hideaway backpack straps.

One Section Carry-on:
Pack exactly like a one-section Pullman (see page 112).

Two Section Carry-on:
Pack like a two-section Pullman (see page 115).

Three Section Carry-on:

1. Pack the largest section, usually the middle, with your heavy and bulky items such as shoes and toiletries. Treat this the same as the bottom layer for the one-section Pullman (see page 112).

2. Use the two smaller sections for interfolded items. This bag is easier to pack if all three sections unzip to open up flat. If not, interfold your clothes with plastic cleaner's bags as shown on page 109 and slide the folded unit into the suitcase. The two outer sections of soft clothing will cushion the inside compartment where you have packed heavy and possibly breakable things.

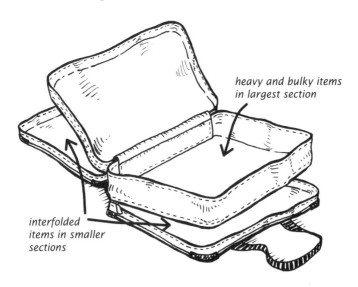

heavy and bulky items
in largest section

interfolded
items in smaller
sections

Packing a Duffel

A duffel is essentially a black hole that will eat your socks if you don't organize things by grouping them. There are two types of duffels — the rectangular (easier to pack) and the round (harder to pack). Both work best for casual clothing and sports gear where wrinkles are not an issue.

Rectangular Duffel

1. This bag opens wide for easy packing but has no interior or exterior pockets or dividers. It is similar to packing a "One-Section Pullman" above, as you will begin by lining the bottom with shoes and other heavy items such as a toiletries kit, cosmetics, and your hair dryer. Fill in any holes with small grouped items or rolled tee-shirts.

2. The next layers must be in self-sealing plastic bags or grouped in containers of some kind. If not, there go those socks — gone until you dump the suitcase upside down. Lisa uses the clear plastic bags that blankets and bedding are sold in; other alternatives are listed on page 164.

   Fill the containers with groups of similar folded or rolled items — for example, tee-shirts in one, underwear in another. Pack grouped items on top of the heavy bottom layer. Now you can lay large items on top — casual pants, sweaters, sweatshirts — folded or rolled to fit.

SMART TRAVEL *Security Update*

Remember: For air travel, the TSA recommends packing shoes last, on top of other contents. See page 94.

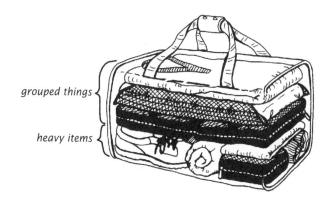

grouped things

heavy items

Round Duffel

This bag is tough to pack because the opening is often narrow. You can test-pack your things as for a rectangular duffel to see if this method works with your bag. If not, try the following packing method:

1. Pack heavy items in the ends of the bag. Group all your small things into containers and place them in the bottom of the bag. Tuck cosmetics and toiletries (in plastic of course) either on top of this layer or in at the ends.

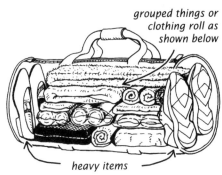

grouped things or clothing roll as shown below

heavy items

2. Place a plastic cleaner's bag on top of your bed. Lay all your clothes out flat on top of the cleaner's bag, starting with the most wrinkle-prone items first. Stack one piece on top of the other, finishing with another cleaner's bag. Now roll, plastic bags and all, starting from the bottom. Pack this tidy package into your duffel.

Create a clothing roll: *Roll.*

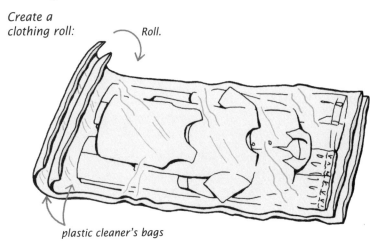

plastic cleaner's bags

Packing a Travel Pack

These combo bags pack like a "One-Section Pullman," using the three-layer strategy:

1. When rolling this bag, place your heaviest things next to the wheels so the weight rests on the wheels, not your arms.

   Pack heavy things opposite the handle if you will be carrying it like a suitcase.

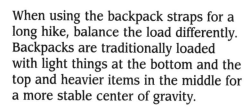

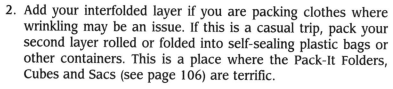

heavy items

When using the backpack straps for a long hike, balance the load differently. Backpacks are traditionally loaded with light things at the bottom and the top and heavier items in the middle for a more stable center of gravity.

If you may be using all three features, pack an evenly balanced load.

2. Add your interfolded layer if you are packing clothes where wrinkling may be an issue. If this is a casual trip, pack your second layer rolled or folded into self-sealing plastic bags or other containers. This is a place where the Pack-It Folders, Cubes and Sacs (see page 106) are terrific.

3. Pack the things you need first on top — layers to beat the weather or your sleeping gear, for example.

DO NOT PACK These Things

According to the TSA and FAA, there are hazardous materials that should not be packed in either a checked bag or your carry-on. Some items used every day may seem harmless, but, when transported by air, can be very dangerous. In flight, variations in temperature and pressure can cause items to leak, generate toxic fumes, or start a fire. Note: These rules are for domestic flights only. For international flights you must contact an airline representative.

Do not pack the following items:

1. Fireworks: signal flares, sparklers or other explosives
2. Flammable liquids or solids: fuel, paints, lighter refills, matches
3. Household items: drain cleaners and solvents
4. Pressurized containers: spray cans, butane fuel, scuba tanks, propane tanks, CO2 cartridges, self-inflating rafts
5. Weapons: firearms, ammunition, gunpowder, mace, tear gas or pepper spray
6. Other hazardous materials: dry ice, gasoline-powered tools, wet-cell batteries, camping equipment with fuel, radioactive materials, poisons, infectious substances

The exceptions:

Some sporting equipment, hazardous materials for personal care or medical needs, and items to support physically challenged passengers can be carried on board.

1. Personal care items containing hazardous materials (e.g., flammable perfume, butane fuel, aerosols) totaling no more than 70 ounces may be carried on board. Contents of each container may not exceed 16 fluid ounces.
2. Matches and lighters may only be carried on your person. However, "strike-anywhere" matches, lighters with flammable liquid reservoirs, and lighter fluid are forbidden.
3. Firearms and ammunition may not be carried by a passenger on an aircraft. However, unloaded firearms may be transported in checked luggage if declared to the agent at check-in and packed in a suitable container. Handguns must be in a locked container. Boxed, small arms ammunition for personal use may be transported in checked luggage. Amounts may vary depending on the airline.
4. Dry ice (4 pounds or less) for packing perishables may be carried on board an aircraft provided the package is vented.
5. Electric wheelchairs must be transported in accordance with airline requirements. The battery may need to be dismounted.
6. As of 1/1/08, lithium batteries may be placed in checked baggage only if installed in electronic devices, or in carry on baggage if installed or stored in a plastic bag or the original retail packaging.

Further restrictions may apply to the above items. Some items may be shipped as air cargo. If in doubt, ask your airline representative.

CHAPTER 12

Packing for Airport Security

PAY ATTENTION TO THIS!

Read this chapter as a reminder before packing for each trip. Some of the following is a recap of information from other chapters in this book. Follow the references for more in-depth discussion and details.

What to Know Before Arriving at the Airport

There are increased passenger and baggage security screenings. Although airports are managed independently, in the US the Transportation Security Administration (TSA) is the federal agency in charge of security so methods are standardized.

1. Current luggage check-in procedures.

- Security screening of all checked baggage for explosives is now in place at all airports. (See pages 93-96 for checked-bag packing tips).

- Curbside luggage check-in is often the best way to avoid long front-counter check-in lines. Call your airline to verify that this service is available.

- There is heightened vigilance for identifying and confiscating unattended bags. Do not leave bags unattended.

- Bags must be **unlocked** to allow for possible manual inspection of contents (see page 94), or use TSA-approved locks.

- Airlines are diligently enforcing checked bag number, size, and weight policies. Call your airline before packing for details (see page 94).

- You must check your bags yourself, and show your current government-issued photo identification (driver's license or passport). Every traveler over the age of 18 must have a photo ID (see page 94).

2. Understand the airport security process.

- Airport security is serious business and applies to every member of the family, including babies.

- Begin at home with a **thorough** search of every carry-on item, including a child's backpack. No toy guns or knives will be allowed. No sharp objects of any kind or size will be allowed through security checkpoints — including scissors, corkscrews, multipurpose tools, etc. They will be confiscated. If you want or need these items at your destination, pack them in your checked luggage. See www.tsa.gov for a current list of items that are not allowed in carry-on baggage.

- Only ticketed passengers holding a valid boarding pass may go through the security checkpoint.

- According to the TSA, passengers on domestic flights are **limited to one carry-on bag** not to exceed 45 linear inches (length + width + height), **plus one personal item** such as a purse, laptop, or briefcase.

- Airports advise checking your bags to minimize your wait at security checkpoints. The more you carry on, the more time it takes to get through security screening.

- Increased security takes more time, so airlines advise arriving **at least 1½ hours in advance** for domestic flights, 2 hours in advance for international flights. Allow more time for peak hours or holiday travel. Lines are longest at the security checkpoints at peak travel times, so allow even more time.

- **Every** passenger must pass through airport security and personal items must be scanned. Prepare children for this process so they are not frightened. If you don't know what to expect, call your airline and ask for details.

3. Make security checkpoints fast and easy.

In addition to electronic scanning of baggage, security checkpoint guards will randomly open and check bags. To speed this process:

- **Go directly to the security checkpoint.** Lines build in seconds, so don't get caught with too little time to clear security. Use airport services inside the secure area.

- **Make bathroom stops before entering the security line.** Your family must stay together and the wait may be long.

- **Pack a healthy dose of patience** plus a book or magazine to pass the waiting time.

- **Pack carry-on bags so contents are easily examined.** Use containers to group items to speed hand checking. Fill the main compartment first; avoid packing in small pockets as this increases screening time.

- **Follow the TSA "3-1-1" rule for carrying on cosmetics, toiletries, and all liquids, gels or aerosols:**
  3= 3 ounce or smaller containers of liquids or gels
  1= 1qt-size clear plastic, zip-top bag to hold 3-oz containers
  1= 1 bag per traveler placed in the security bin for screening

- **Move through the screening equipment, now set to lower tolerances, as quickly as possible.** Empty pockets of unnecessary coins or keys, avoid large metal belt buckles or jewelry, and leave extra jewelry at home or pack it in a checked bag. Place your wallet and jewelry in a carry-on when passing through the screening station so they will be X-rayed.

- **Pack undeveloped film in carry-on bags only.**

- **Be ready to remove your shoes and coat** and pass them through the screening machine. You may also be subjected to hand-held metal detector wand searches and pat downs.

- **Check for all your belongings before leaving the screening area!** Wallets, keys and coins, jewelry, cell phones — even laptops — are often forgotten.

4. Minimize Screening Time.

- **Pack metal items in a checked bag** or place them in your carry-on. Scanning equipment reads a total of the metal on you. Buttons, zippers, hair accessories, and shoe fittings and shanks may add up to wand and pat-down searches.

- **Don't wear** a bra with an underwire to avoid wand and hand pat-down searches.

- **Limit electronic equipment** (cell phones, pagers, games, CD players, etc.). Place those you take in your carry-on. You need to prove that they work, so have batteries installed.

- **Remove laptops from bag for X-raying separately.**

- **Don't wrap gifts** as they may be searched, and confiscated. Pack in a checked bag or plan to wrap upon arrival.

PART III:
CUSTOMIZE YOUR WARDROBE

Some trips require specialized clothing and packing tips.

See what experienced travelers recommend.

CHAPTER 13

Packing for Business Travel

When dollars count, don't leave anything out!

When you consider that you will never get a second chance to make a good first impression, it's obvious that careful wardrobe planning is the key to a successful business trip. Of all the kinds of trips you might take in your lifetime, business travel requires the most careful consideration — it's about your livelihood.

Appearance counts! Etch this into your mind. Dressing for business is not about wearing what you feel like wearing; it is about wearing what you must to get the job done and make the best impression. If you travel in sweats and your business contact unexpectedly meets you at the airport, it will take a lot of suit-and-starched-shirt days to change this too-casual image. Your travel and business attire should convey responsibility and professionalism at all times.

Decide What to Take

Less is best — pack the smallest amount possible to be well-dressed. Traveling with carry-on luggage for a short trip is the most efficient use of your time, but as the airlines continue to limit the size and number of carry-on pieces this becomes more difficult. Some frequent business travelers pack very light but have laundry done daily in the hotel. This is an expensive yet efficient alternative to packing more. (Be sure to read "Checking or Carrying Bags?" beginning on page 93.)

For a trip of more than three days in one location, consider packing more and checking your baggage. There is a trade-off between maximizing work time and being willing to wait for bags because you need more clothing to be professionally presentable.

Do not travel in anything you cannot wear for business! Just imagine arriving without your luggage and having to do business wearing jeans in a suit culture. If you plan to check your luggage, travel in appropriate business clothing and carry your toiletries, cosmetics, and a change of shirt/blouse and underwear with you.

Daytime Business Wardrobe Options

Follow these easy steps to plan your daytime travel wardrobe:

1. **Use your itinerary to plan a calendar** (see page 10) and assign clothing notes to each event.

Monday 3rd	Tuesday 4th	Wednesday 5th
7a.m. *fly to Denver* *(formal suit)* *go directly to* *2 p.m. meeting* *6 p.m. cocktails* *& dinner*	*8 a.m.* *at office* *casual - no tie* *hands on* *no dinner plans*	*7a.m.* *breakfast meeting* *(formal suit)* *9:30 presentation* *3 p.m. fly home*

2. **Know the business customs and culture** of the place you are visiting. For example, the business uniform of Singapore (depending on the industry) is an open-collared, short-sleeved dress shirt with dress pants — and a coat and tie only if you're meeting with the company president. Don't try this in Tokyo though, where white shirt, tie, and dark suit are the only accepted uniform. Conversely, in Phoenix some men (even conservative bankers) wear short-sleeved shirts and cowboy boots with their suits. Women generally wear suits or conservative dresses plus pantyhose for business attire around the world, even in 110°F weather. If you are unsure about the appropriate business attire for your destination, ask the people you'll be meeting or a colleague who has been there before.

Your type of business and the business activities planned during your stay also set the tone for dress. Hands-on projects require more casual dress, while sales presentations to the president of the company will call for your most formal business attire.

You can't go wrong in a suit, dress shirt, and tie for men; a conservative dress or a suit with a simple blouse, sheer hose and mid-heel pump is a safe bet for women. You might be a bit overdressed, but it is always best to err on the conservative side.

Conservative Business Attire
You can't go wrong with these!

3. **Decide on the type and number of outfits to take,** using your calendar notes as a guide. If you will be in the same location with the same people for the entire trip, you will need to take more outfits or plan for lots of mixing and matching (see pages 24-25). If you'll be seeing different people every day, theoretically you could take only one outfit. But what would you do if you spilled coffee down the front of your suit?

Menswear experts feel strongly that both pieces of a suit must be worn and cleaned together or the fabrics will no longer match. Women generally pay less and expect less wear from a suit and so feel more free to interchange suit pieces with other things.

Use the following versatile wardrobe pieces as a guide when choosing items from your closet to build a business travel wardrobe.

Three-day Trip, Conservative Business Wardrobe:

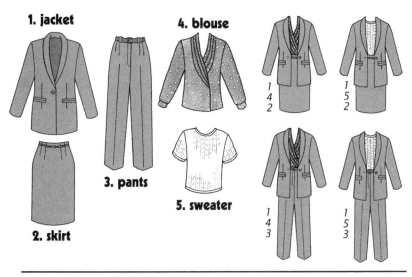

One Week Trip, Casual Business Wardrobe:

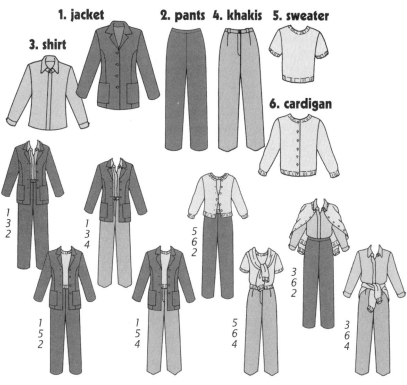

1. jacket   2. pants   4. khakis   5. sweater

3. shirt

6. cardigan

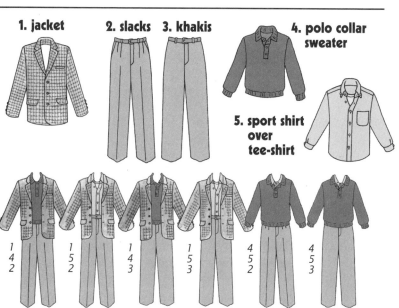

1. jacket   2. slacks   3. khakis   4. polo collar sweater

5. sport shirt over tee-shirt

After-Hours Business Wardrobe Options

If your business travel days include after-hours functions, you may find yourself wearing the same clothes all day or you may want to plan for a change. You may also need other clothing for personal plans. Consider the following:

- Business deals are often finalized during dinner. Do you have a change of clothes or accessories that will take you to an elegant, expense-account restaurant or to a dressed-down, more casual dinner? If your day begins with a breakfast meeting and ends with cocktails and dinner with no time to change, is your suit up to the test or will you be a wrinkled mess? Long days require the most wrinkle-resistant clothing you can acquire.

- Smart, casual attire may be called for if the after-hours get-togethers will have a more relaxed attitude. Do you need to pack a well-coordinated casual outfit?

- A workout before or after a day of meetings is the perfect stress reducer. Does your hotel have exercise facilities or a pool? Pack the appropriate clothing and shoes. Look for high-tech, quick-drying athletic wear so you can pack only one set and hand wash it after each use. In addition to your swimsuit, don't forget that many health club or hotel pools require the use of a swim cap. Pack a cover-up to wear to the pool and rubber thongs that can double as slippers in your room.

- Will you have a night off to relax in your room, order room service, and watch TV? I always make space for a robe and slippers or sweats for those decadent evenings.

Shoes, Accessories and The Extras

Shoes and accessories can make or break your business look and require careful planning to get you through your trip.

1. **Limit shoes to no more than three pairs.** They're the heaviest and bulkiest items to pack. Wear one pair, pack two. Choose from these, depending on the formality of your workplace.

For winter weather where boots are required, paring down on other shoes is a necessity for light travel. Consider packing a pair of plastic boots that slip over your shoes to keep your feet dry instead of bulky winter boots.

SMART TRAVEL

Jeff equates the number of suits and shoes to take with the length of the trip. For a one-week trip he takes two suits, so two pair of shoes.

2. **Take accessories that pack a punch** when it comes to changing the look of an outfit. Ties for men and scarves and jewelry for women are the smallest items to pack. The suit "goes away" and the accessories become the focal point when you pair a different shirt/blouse each day with an interesting tie or scarf. Suits take up lots of room, accessories very little. (See page 53 for some interesting ways to tie a scarf.)

3. **Buy a briefcase that complements your clothing.** Choose one in the best quality you can afford so it will take daily abuse and still look presentable. In addition to work papers, use your briefcase as a closet away from home — make sure there is room for a change of shirts or accessories.

   For women, avoid carrying a large handbag in addition to your briefcase or tote bag. Instead, carry your personal items in a small purse that you can tuck into your bigger bag. Choose one that will work for daytime activities as well as evening engagements.

4. **Be prepared for weather changes.** Tuck an umbrella into your briefcase or tote bag. Gloves are lifesavers too. Carry your raincoat on the plane to save on suitcase space. A medium-weight raincoat is perfect for just about anywhere but Alaska in December, especially if you plan to dash from taxi to office. Gloves and a hat pack small but deliver a lot of warmth. Layering clothing is a great strategy for handling extremes and swings in temperature.

SMART TRAVEL

David keeps a business card for identification in the pocket of his raincoat in case he leaves it on the airplane or someone grabs the wrong tan coat off the rack.

5. **Pack your travel alarm clock.** Don't plan on hotel wake-up calls to get you up on time and don't count on the hotel having an alarm clock — that works — in your room. Take charge with a clock that you know works properly and that will wake you on time (see page 197).

SMART TRAVEL

Barbara W. always puts a fresh battery in her travel alarm before she leaves home so she's sure it won't give out in the middle of the night before an important morning meeting. It eliminates restless nights spent worrying about oversleeping!

SMART TRAVEL

Frequent travelers take what they need to feel at home wherever they are — family photos, for example. I can't imagine starting my morning without coffee so I pack an immersion heater, plastic mug, and instant coffee.

ALWAYS PACKED AND READY TO GO

You can speed your packing and eliminate frustration if you keep some things travel-ready at all times.

- Prepare a cosmetics bag or toiletries travel kit and buy a travel set of hair-care appliances. Store these with your packing supplies so they're ready to go when you are. Be sure you refill and replenish supplies immediately upon your return.

- Keep extras of the things you are prone to forget with your luggage. I always keep a swimsuit in my suitcase so I know I'll be able to swim or use the spa without having to buy an expensive new swimsuit in the hotel shop.

- Place a supply of business cards in a self-sealing plastic bag in your suitcase — in case you forget to pack extras or run out.

Business Luggage

If you are a frequent business traveler or plan to become one, you should have a wardrobe of luggage that will take you on trips of varying lengths. Your first purchase should be a good-quality, carry-on or wheel-aboard bag, preferably a 22" or smaller. (See "Choosing the Right Luggage" beginning on page 79 for in-depth information about luggage choices and recommendations.) Many business travelers prefer a garment bag but, due to new airline regulations for carry-ons, this category may no longer meet the size requirements.

Do not take your old sports bag as business luggage. Invest in quality luggage that will travel well and enhance your image. Remember the line about making a good first impression? If business people meet you at the airport or if you take your bags to an office upon arrival or before departure, your luggage becomes part of the impression you create. Choose a dark color so soil is less noticeable. It's nice to have a matched set of luggage, but since "fashion" colors in luggage change constantly, that isn't always possible unless you buy it all at one time or choose black.

Here are some key considerations for choosing business luggage:

- **Buy a briefcase that will hold your laptop computer.** Make sure your purse will fit in your briefcase/computer bag. This strategy will help minimize the number of carry-on pieces. This bag should fit under the seat in front of you. To avoid being an easy mark for computer theft — unfortunately on the rise in airports and other common traveler's locales — it's a good idea to use a bag that doesn't look like a typical computer bag.

- **Choose your luggage carefully.** On domestic airlines, length + height + depth must equal no more than 45", including the handles and wheels. (See page 99 for more information.)

- **Make sure your carry-on is easy for you to lift or small enough to fit under the seat in front of you** on an airplane. Unless you are traveling first class (even then it isn't easy), it is almost impossible to put a wheel-aboard bag under the seat in front of you. The space under the seat may be large enough, but the rows are too close together to get the bag underneath. Also remember that separate luggage carts must now be stored under the seat, not in the overhead storage.

Necessities

As you travel more and more on business, you'll probably begin to make a list of the little things that make a big difference in conducting business on the road. Nancy D. wouldn't be without her travel desk accessories kit. Bill P. always packs his power supply and phone cords for his laptop computer first, so he doesn't forget them. Some other things for an efficient business trip might include:

- **All frequent flyer, frequent renter, or guest numbers** listed in one easy-to-locate place. Include toll-free numbers for airline reservations, particularly those for elite status frequent flyers.

- **Certificates for travel upgrades and hotel and car discount certificates.** If you're a member of AAA, AARP, or another organization that offers special traveler's discounts, be sure you have your cards with you.

- **Plenty of business cards.** David reminds us this applies to international travel too. For an international destination, have your business card translated into the local language and be sure to carry an adequate supply of the right ones with you.

- **Batteries for all of your equipment.** They can be hard to find, so take extras or a recharger.

- **Indispensable little office products.** A highlighter, yellow stickies — all those indispensable items you depend on — should have a permanent home in your briefcase. Keep them organized in a self-sealing plastic bag.

At Trip's End

At the end of your trip, make written notes on your packing list about what you packed and wore. If the blue shirt looked great but wrinkled terribly, make a note so you won't mistakenly pack that shirt again.

On the homeward plane trip, I don't give myself permission to read my novel until I have done my expenses, written thank you notes and trip reports, and evaluated my clothing choices. An executive I know can tell from her trip recap files what she has worn to every business presentation during her career. Now that's very complete note taking!

Business Travel Packing List

Use this list of categories to create your own personal packing list. See page 50 for a more complete list of clothing. Be as specific as possible: list and describe each item, i.e. blue long-sleeved dress shirt. Make two copies of your list — one to leave at home and one to carry with your other business documents.

- Appropriate selection of daytime business attire

- After-hours clothing

- Ample accessories (ties and scarves especially) to change the look of your business clothes

- Clothing for weather changes (raincoat and umbrella, gloves, plastic over-the-shoe boots)

- A good briefcase or tote bag

- Dependable alarm clock

- Workout clothes

- Comfy, in-room clothing

- Things that make you happy

Chapter 14

Packing for a Cruise

Educated choices here are critical — once the ship sails everything is "set in stone."

Some travelers consider a cruise the ultimate vacation. It's great to be pampered on a self-contained vessel with all the amenities. As with any other mode of travel, taking the right clothes results in a more enjoyable trip.

Step 1: Choose the Right Ship

The most important cruise decision you'll make is choosing the ship that is right for you. According to Rosemary, a staff member who lived on board a cruise ship ten months a year, travelers must communicate their cruise expectations to their travel agent so they can be matched up with the ship of their dreams. Some cruise lines are more formal and require more formal dress and some are quite casual; some provide 24-hour action and some are very quiet and relaxing. Choose one that suits your travel style and cruise expectations.

Step 2: Pack the Right Clothes

Deciding what to wear on a cruise is directly related to the cruise line and ship you have chosen, plus your destinations. A Caribbean cruise calls for warm-weather clothing for beach activities and shore excursions plus dressier things for evenings on board. A cruise along European rivers may require casual clothes for daily touring and dressy attire for dinner.

You may want to pack more for a cruise than for a vacation of the same duration where you're always on the move. You'll be seeing the same people every day and you won't have to handle your luggage much, if at all, so "packing light" may not be an issue.

Most cruise lines send out a brochure that includes a list of suggested clothing along with confirmation of your trip. Cruise lines also have websites and fax-back services that provide detailed dress suggestions for each ship and itinerary, laundry and dry cleaning price lists, and even menus.

The main difference between a cruise and general travel is that once you are on board, you are there. Unpack upon arrival, pack at the end of the cruise to go home. Pure heaven! Good-bye to a different hotel every night! Cruise lines generally don't have a baggage limitation, but airlines do. The real limitation is closet size on board the ship and they are notoriously small. Don't even dream that your room and closet will be the size of those in the movies.

SMART TRAVEL

A word to the wise from Liz — on her cruise to Alaska on a small ship she was allowed only one bag. Check your cruise line information for a baggage limitation before you plan your cruise wardrobe.

Some ships will store large suitcases once you are on board to provide more space in your stateroom, but most bags fit under the bed. For long cruises, it is possible to send extra bags to the ship in advance to avoid airline baggage restrictions.

Daytime Cruise Attire

"Resort casual" for day is the general rule on board most ships. This includes Bermuda-length shorts or pants and blouses and sundresses for women and Bermuda-length shorts, casual khaki pants, slacks and sport shirts, polo or tee-shirts for men. Jeans are OK on most cruise lines but tank tops, cut-offs, and jeans with holes are not acceptable. Pack clothing with expandable or very loose waistlines, as excellent and plentiful food is a highlight of cruising. A warm-weather, daytime wardrobe appears on the next page.

For ideas for a casual, cool-weather cruise wardrobe, see page 24.

Clothing for On-Shore Activities

Shore excursions call for dressing for the activity or for the destination. If you are going to a beach, be sure to take your sunscreen and hat and wear a cover-up over your swimsuit. Clothing appropriate for the ship may be too bare for conservative areas toured on excursions. Men may be required to wear long pants, and at some religious sites women must have their arms and legs covered.

Modest dresses that cover the shoulders and arms and have longer skirts are good choices, as are casual pants and a blouse. I often tuck a large, lightweight cotton scarf into my tote bag that can be used as a shawl or head covering. (See page 39.)

Daytime Attire

Evening Wear On Board

With the increasing appeal of cruises plus the casual dressing trend, cruising is more casual today than ever. This means a more relaxed approach to dressing, even for dinner. Except for longer cruises with formal nights, you will seldom need a gown or tuxedo. On two- or three-day cruises, dressing for dinner on a "casual evening" can mean something as simple as changing from your shorts to a nice pair of pants. The ship's daily newspaper will indicate the "Suggested Dress of the Evening" during your cruise.

Casual Evening Attire

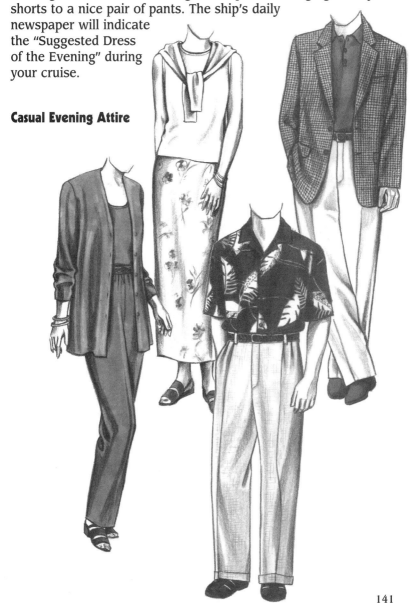

141

Informal, Semi-Formal, or Smart Casual Evening

These terms suggest a sport coat or blazer with slacks for the men, preferably with a tie — or a suit and tie. For women, a pretty dress or dressy pantsuit is appropriate. Rosemary recommends a "little black dress" as the perfect thing to wear several times with different jewelry, jackets, scarves, and other accessories.

Formal Evening Dress

This can be a dark business suit with tie for men and cocktail dress or dressy pantsuit for women. If you love to dress up and are willing to pack a tuxedo or dinner jacket or a long evening gown, please to do so. Many people do and find it to be the high point of the cruise. Don't own a tux? You can rent one on board some ships for a flat fee for the length of the cruise. Just let your travel agent or cruise line know in advance and it will be hanging in your closet when you arrive. No packing! You will also be perfectly attired if you choose the suit/cocktail dress option.

Cruise Clothes at a Glance

Versatile clothing items in easy-care fabrics that can be dressed up or down are the best choices for men and women. Here are some suggestions for three- and seven-day cruises.

Woman's Three-day Cruise Wardrobe, with Casual Evenings:

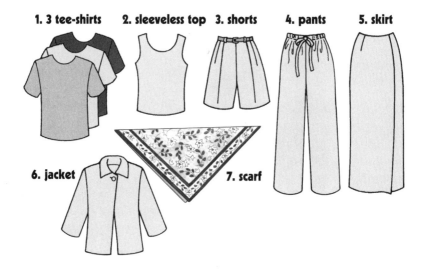

1. 3 tee-shirts   2. sleeveless top   3. shorts   4. pants   5. skirt

6. jacket   7. scarf

DAY 1   DAY 2   DAY 3

Day   Eve   Day   Eve   Day   Eve

Add for Seven-day to Unlimited Cruise:

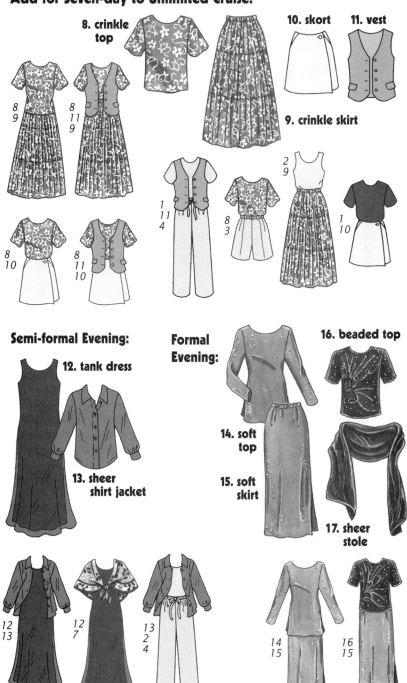

8. crinkle top

10. skort

11. vest

8 9

8 11 9

9. crinkle skirt

2 9

8 10

8 11 10

1 11 4

8 3

1 10

Semi-formal Evening:

12. tank dress

13. sheer shirt jacket

Formal Evening:

14. soft top

15. soft skirt

16. beaded top

17. sheer stole

12 13

12 7

13 2 4

14 15

16 15

Men's Three-day Cruise, with Casual Evenings:

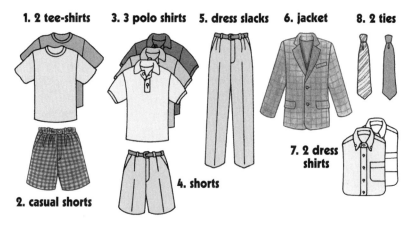

1. 2 tee-shirts   3. 3 polo shirts   5. dress slacks   6. jacket   8. 2 ties

7. 2 dress shirts

4. shorts

2. casual shorts

DAY 1		DAY 2		DAY 3	
Day	Eve	Day	Eve	Day	Eve

SMART TRAVEL Tip

For me, the worst possible clothing disaster would be if my luggage did not make the ship. I suggest traveling to your cruise departure city in something comfortable with a change of clothing, a swimsuit, and your necessities in your carry-on bag. If your second outfit will interchange with what you are wearing, your luggage may have a chance to catch up with you before you have to resort to buying new clothing in the shops on board!

Add for Seven-day to Unlimited Cruise:

9. 2 sports shirts   **11. casual pants**   **7. 3rd shirt**   **8. 3rd tie**

10. shorts

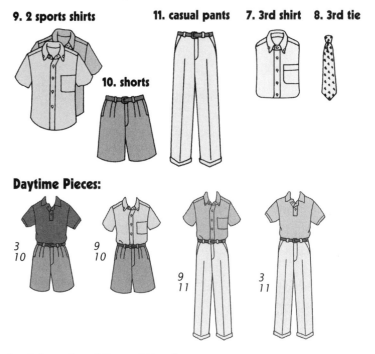

Daytime Pieces:

3
10

9
10

9
11

3
11

Semi-formal and Formal Evening:

6
7
8
5

Bring a suit and/or a tuxedo.

Plan Ahead

All ships have laundry services (some also have self-service laundries) and most have dry cleaning too, so you can plan to wash underwear and a few clothing items partway through the trip. Check with your cruise line about packing a travel iron; some consider them a fire hazard. Irons are usually available in the self-service laundry and you can also have things professionally pressed on board.

Necessities

As with almost any other kind of trip, there are some things you definitely don't want to be caught without on a cruise.

Clothing Items

- **Sun hat, visor, and lots of sunscreen.** There are no shade trees on the ship.

- **At least two swimsuits.** Take one suit to wear and one to dry, plus rubber-soled shoes to wear to the pool.

- **Cover-ups.** Walking around the ship in just a swimsuit is not allowed. Shirt and shorts or a beach robe for men, and sarongs, oversized shirts, or beach robes for women are all suggested. I like a sarong because it takes almost no space in my luggage and can be worn as a skirt, dress, or shawl. Buy sarongs in swimwear departments and shops or ethnic clothing shops or make your own. Sarongs come in different sizes and can be tied many ways. What works best for you depends on your body size.

- **Comfortable, flat, rubber-soled walking shoes.** You'll need these to wear on deck and for shore excursions.

- **A light wrap.** Wear in overly air-conditioned rooms and for strolling on deck after dinner (for women, a shawl, jacket or sweater; for men, a sweater, sport coat, or jacket are suggested).

- **Exercise clothing.** Indulge in that fabulous dessert buffet without guilt!

- **Special clothing and accessories for cruise theme nights.** Check your advance information for what and when. A Hawaiian shirt that can be worn for casual day can also become your "Polynesian Night" costume.

Other Handy Cruise Items

- **A day pack or tote bag** for the pool and shore trips — perfect for carrying your water bottle, camera and film, umbrella, sunscreen, insect repellent, and windbreaker or sweater. (This can also double as your airline carry-on bag.)

- **Adequate supply of any medications** for the entire trip. Even though ships have doctors and pharmacies, they may not carry your type of medication.

- **A voltage converter** if recommended in the ship brochure. Ships have different electrical supply systems, depending on where they were built and the countries they serve. Some provide hair dryers in each stateroom; others may have them available upon request.

- **Extensions cord or outlet "expander."** Cruise ship cabins typically have only two outlets by the desk/vanity table — one 110V and one 220V (see pages 194-195). Use the 220V outlet for a dual voltage appliance with a plug adaptor. Reserve the 110V for the outlet "expander" for such items as a rechargeable video camera or cell phone. Bathroom outlets are strictly for electric shavers.

- **Binoculars** for viewing sites from on deck or shore excursions

- **Personal CD or MP3 player, or a portable radio** for tuning into the unique sounds of the countries you visit

- **Reading materials for the length of your trip,** or plan to make a visit to the ship library at the very beginning of your cruise; otherwise, the selection will be picked over.

- **Motion sickness medication** or wristbands (Sea Bands®) available in drugstores. Ask your doctor about prescription choices before you leave.

- **Hard-to-find items** such as a special toothpaste, queen-sized pantyhose, your favorite mints

SMART TRAVEL

Linda Coffman of CruiseDiva.com (see page 239) suggests a day pack or tote bag for carrying things off the ship on debarkation day. Luggage is picked up during the last night of the cruise. Passengers must save an outfit to wear off the ship and will want to pack last minute toiletry items in this bag.

CHAPTER 15

Packing for Adventure Travel

Sometimes you can't shop, so plan ahead. Off-the-beaten-path problem-solving is critical here, so go prepared for every possibility.

The best clothing for adventure travel does the right job for the trip without any fuss. Go to your favorite travel shops, sporting goods or outdoor store, or review the merchandise in mail-order and on-line catalogs for the best in high-tech fabrics and straightforward clothing and gear that will withstand the rigors of your trip.

Do Your Packing Homework

If you are traveling with a group, study the materials sent from your tour operator. Often, there are strict guidelines for luggage size (small and flexible) and weight (light!). You may be taking various types of transportation where stowing gear in a small space is essential. For some destinations, there are also rigid guidelines for clothing colors and fabrics. Advance materials sent to June S. for her wilderness safari to Botswana specifically stated, *"Bright colors and white are not advised and army camouflage uniforms or army hats are forbidden"* (their emphasis).

Tour operators are the experts who know what works and what is needed for a comfortable trip to your destination any time of the year. Elaine's guide on her trip to Tibet and Nepal warned, "Landslides are common in these rugged countries so be prepared to carry your own bags!" It is wise to follow any "suggested equipment lists" the tour operator sends prior to your trip. They will also tell you what laundry facilities are available. If they don't, be sure to ask.

SMART TRAVEL

Lisa bought inexpensive khaki clothing that was required for a safari and simply left these items at her last stop in Africa. They were not colors or items she would wear again and she knew they would be appreciated by the local people.

If you are traveling independently, your best sources of information are personal accounts of travelers who have been before you as well as travel guidebooks and information gleaned from the internet. Every destination is unique and therefore different, but there are similarities too.

Adventure Travel Basics

No matter what your destination, you'll need clothing that packs small and light and is comfortable in a wide range of weather conditions. You must pack everything with you that you will need for the trip. Laundry facilities will be few and far between; search out clothing that can be washed out in a sink or basin, hung to dry overnight, and worn the next day. Look for Supplex nylon (see page 71), Cordura nylon, textured nylon, or a fabric description that indicates key words or phrases, including:

- lightweight
- feels like cotton but dries fast
- packs flat
- can be washed out and hung to dry overnight
- moisture-wicking fabric

1. **Pants.** Two pair of cotton-like Supplex or Cordura nylon pants (one to wear and a spare) will take you on a trip of any length. Cotton jeans or canvas casual pants are not recommended as they are much bulkier to pack and take forever to dry.

SMART TRAVEL *Item*

Several manufacturers make long pants that convert to shorts. You simply zip off the legs (the zipper hides under a clever tuck in the pant leg). When changing clothes is not an option, these pants are very practical for cold mornings that turn into hot days and for warm days that become mosquito-filled evenings. (www.exofficio.com)

2. **Shorts.** If you are going to a very hot climate, take one pair of nylon shorts and one pair of nylon long pants. You should be able to wash these shorts at night and put them on the next morning. Choose shorts with longer leg styles for men and women — for protection from the elements as well as modesty in conservative cultures.

3. **Skirt.** Women may want to pack a modest, longer skirt or a divided skirt (culottes) in place of shorts for travel in very conservative hot-weather countries.

4. **Long-sleeved shirt.** Choose a tightly woven fabric that will protect against sun and insects. You can wear it by itself or layer it over or under other things. The ideal shirt has roll-up shirt-sleeve tabs that turn long sleeves into short to add temperature flexibility.

SMART TRAVEL *Item*

Special sunblock clothing with an SPF of 30+ is available for those who really shouldn't be in the sun but want to be outside. A typical summer shirt provides only an SPF 5-9, so specially treated sunblock clothing provides great added protection. Shirts, pants, hats, and jackets are among the many items available. Clothing can repel insects, too! Look for BUZZ OFF™ — insect shield protection that is built into clothing, not put on your skin (www.exofficio.com)

5. **Tee-shirts.** Tee-shirts that are easy to wash and quick to dry and are made of high-tech wicking fabrics (see pages 72 and 75) are the best. Pack a couple of these shirts in colors you love to brighten up your basic bottoms. Most versatile is a short-sleeved tee-shirt so take at least two. Add a long-sleeved tee-shirt or turtleneck for colder weather plus a sleeveless shirt for really hot times. Any of these can be layered under other pieces.

6. **Underwear.** High-tech saves the day. Fabrics made from synthetic fibers that wick will keep your body comfortable all day. Wash them at night and they'll be dry by morning. Take just two pair — one to wear and a spare (perfect for any minimal luggage trip, including business travel). If you are headed to an area where cold weather is a possibility, take a pair of wicking-fabric or silk long underwear to layer under your clothes or to use for sleepwear.

7. **Socks.** If you're still wearing cotton socks, go to a travel shop or sporting goods store and investigate high-tech sport socks. Look for specially cushioned socks for walking, for hiking, and for running; most are made of wicking synthetic fibers. Read the labels carefully, then buy and try one pair before investing in several. You're the only one who knows what feels best on your feet. Test wash and dry the ones you like best before traveling with them. The number of pairs you need to pack will depend on how fast the socks dry; if they dry overnight (the best kind), you may pack just two pair.

8. **Outerwear.** Be prepared for rain, cool nights, chilly high altitude, or unexpected cold snaps by packing gear to layer for comfort. Long underwear will help, but you can also layer with the clothing mentioned above. A sleeveless tee-shirt under a short-sleeved tee-shirt under the long-sleeved shirt might be all you'll need. A layer for colder weather, such as a microfleece "sweater," that will pack smaller than a traditional sweatshirt or sweater is perfect. Top that with a windproof/water-resistant jacket (I like one with a hood) and you are set. As always, a hat and gloves take up little space and will go a very long way toward keeping you comfortable.

9. **Shoes.** The type of shoes you take will vary, depending completely on your destination. If you have space, take two pair of your daily shoes so that you can alternate to allow the shoes to dry completely between wearings. That will also give you

dry shoes to wear after a rainstorm or an unexpected fall in a creek. Some other thoughts on shoes: Don't forget a pair of rubber thongs to wear in the shower or for swimming and consider lightweight wool clogs or comfortable sandals (temperature will dictate) for wear "in camp."

Beyond Clothing: Some Sanity Savers

People often don't think to pack these useful items:

- **Insect repellent.** An absolute necessity! See page 211 for complete information.

- **Sunscreen**

- **Bandanna.** This little item has a thousand uses. One of the best is to tie it over your nose and mouth to filter out dust. You can also use one for a face cloth, hand towel, napkin, placemat, seat cover, headband, head scarf, or sleep mask. Take at least two; your companions will want to borrow yours.

- **Tissues for every possible use,** particularly ill-equipped bathrooms

BACK COUNTRY CLOTHES CARE

Since you may be doing a little hand laundry every night, don't forget to pack the right tools to make the task as painless and efficient as possible. (For tips on doing the laundry, see "Stay Neat and Clean" beginning on page 184.)

Some basic things to pack for this chore include:

- **Flat rubber sink stopper.** Use when you are fortuniate enough to have a sink!

- **Detergent.** Check with a travel or sporting goods store for biodegradable detergent for back-country use. Some products can be used in hot, cole, or salt water. Steve suggests a chunk of Fels Naptha soap stored in a film canister.

- **Clothesline.** The Flexo-line® (www.magellans.com) holds clothes without clothespins.

- **Hat with an all-around brim and cord** to secure it. A baseball cap is not as effective as a sun protector.

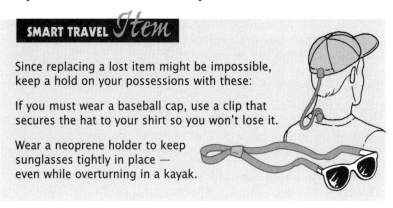

SMART TRAVEL _Item_

Since replacing a lost item might be impossible, keep a hold on your possessions with these:

If you must wear a baseball cap, use a clip that secures the hat to your shirt so you won't lose it.

Wear a neoprene holder to keep sunglasses tightly in place — even while overturning in a kayak.

- **Lots of film and camera batteries**
- **Flashlight with spare batteries and bulb**
- **Water bottle.** Read page 207 to learn about water bottles that will purify local water.

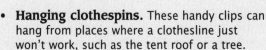

- **Inflatable hangers.** These lightweight hangers inflate to allow air circulation for faster drying; take two.

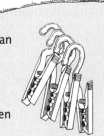

- **Hanging clothespins.** These handy clips can hang from places where a clothesline just won't work, such as the tent roof or a tree.

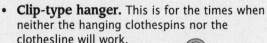

- **Clip-type hanger.** This is for the times when neither the hanging clothespins nor the clothesline will work.

- **Towel and washcloth.** Many cultures do not use washcloths so they do not provide them. Handi-Wipes (disposable towels available in the cleaning or paper supplies at your grocery) can be cut in half, used, and tossed. Viscose rayon towels are also great for travel as they are extremely absorbent and dry very quickly — unlike cotton towels that turn rancid smelling before they're dry! If you cannot find a viscose washcloth, cut a viscose towel into smaller sizes. Look for PackTowl® or Travel Towl™ in travel shops or sporting goods stores. Aquis® is a super-absorbent, poly/nylon towel sold in linen departments. Roll your wet laundry in one of these moisture grabbers to remove excess water, ensuring overnight drying in any climate.

- **Silk sleep sack.** Clean sheets every day are an unlikely luxury in the back country. Slip into your own 100% silk Dream Sack™ (www.dreamsack.com) for a worry-free rest. Machine washable and quick drying, it stuffs into an 8" x 4" x 1" pouch. (www.dreamsack.com)

- **Large plastic trash bag and twist ties.** Use to completely line your suitcase or travel pack if your trip is through dusty or wet territory. Place the trash bag inside your bag and then pack into the trash bag. Secure with a twist tie and close your bag. Or, place your whole bag or pack into a larger trash bag and close with a twist tie.

- **Binoculars**

- **Day pack**

SMART TRAVEL

Lisa's latest hot tip is saving the almost-finished rolls of toilet paper from home to pack on a backwoods camping trip. She flattened the rolls to save space, then took a roll each time she went behind a bush. She tucked the used tissue inside the cardboard roll to dispose of the entire thing in camp.

If ever there was a time to create a packing list and check it carefully, it is now. Adventure travel generally means shopping for a missing item is out of the question. This time you must create your own list. I can't help you out with this one, as each adventure trip is very different from the next.

Packing for a Resort Vacation

Ask about dress codes and plan ahead so that you will always feel welcome.

Whether going to a vacation area such as Hawaii or to a specific destination, such as a golf resort, the goal is to relax and have a great time. I can do that best if I know what to pack. When it comes to resorts, there are some definite guidelines.

Resort Dress Codes

At some resorts you'll be completely comfortable in very casual clothes. At others, you can be casual during the day, but will need conservative, more formal attire for meals. There are many different degrees of formality; call your resort before packing or look at the brochure to see what the people in the photos are wearing.

Many older resorts with a history of formality are slowly relaxing their dress codes, but relaxing them does not mean they don't care what you wear. "City formal" means suit and tie; "resort formal" indicates sport coat and tie — and the relaxed standard may be sport coat without a tie. Some "recommend" but do not require that a jacket be worn for dinner. Many resort dining rooms do not allow jeans or athletic shoes and many request a long-sleeved shirt or a turtleneck for men. Khaki pants are a safe alternative to jeans. Women are always appropriately dressed in dresses, skirts and tops, or in smart pants outfits.

In most resorts, short shorts are for tennis only and longer shorts are suggested for daily wear. At many locations, shorts of any length are *not* proper dinner attire.

If your resort is on the beach or has a swimming pool, pack cover-ups (for men and women) to wear over a swimsuit. When walking from your room to the water and for meals, shoes plus shorts and a shirt, a sarong, a long shirt, or a beach dress are all acceptable attire.

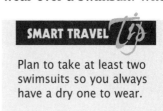

SMART TRAVEL

Plan to take at least two swimsuits so you always have a dry one to wear.

Even though you might think that a beach resort in Hawaii would be very casual, this is not always the case. Marion is the Kahala Club Manager for the Kahala Hotel and Resort, a luxurious beachfront resort in Honolulu. She suggests that in public areas such as the hotel lobby and restaurants the less skin you show the better. Marion recommends all of the above swimsuit cover-ups and adds that, when wearing a sarong, tying it over the top of a two-piece swimsuit covers the most skin.

Marion also suggests "casual elegance" when dining at the Kahala's casual beachfront café. In the more formal restaurant upstairs, the hotel dress code specifies a shirt with a collar, long pants, and shoes for men. Women will want to pack dresses, skirts and tops, or smart pants outfits to be appropriately dressed. The "shirt with a collar and long pants" dress code for men is very common at resorts in North America and indicates that shorts and a tee-shirt are pool attire, not dining room attire.

Casual, Comfortable Resort Wear

No matter where you're headed, here are some resort wear ideas that are acceptable everywhere. It is always best to pack conservatively; you can dress more casually once you are there and see the local tone. These suggestions are unisex, with additions for women.

For a warm-weather day:

- shirt with a collar
- longer shorts
- athletic shoes or sandals
- plus sundress or casual skirt and blouse for women

For a warm-weather evening:

- shirt with a collar
- khakis or dress slacks
- loafers
- sweater, sport coat, or blazer
- pants outfit for women
- dress or skirt and blouse for women

For a cold-weather day:

- shirt and turtleneck
- khaki pants or jeans
- athletic shoes or casual boots
- sweater, jacket, fleece vest, or pullover
- casual dress or skirt and sweater for women

For a cold-weather evening:

- shirt or turtleneck
- khaki pants or dress slacks
- street shoes or dress boots
- sweater, sport coat, or blazer
- pants outfit for women
- dress or skirt and sweater for women

When traveling to a resort outside your home country, always consider the local culture if you will be leaving the resort grounds. (See "Worldwide Wardrobing," beginning on page 36.)

If sports activities are a focal point of the resort, knowing what is available before you arrive is important. If there is horseback riding and you want to participate, pack your riding clothes. Sporting equipment is often available for guest use or for rent, so this is an ideal time to try out a new challenge.

CHAPTER 17

Packing for Sports Travel

Traveling today often includes taking sports equipment.
Sometimes that means "special handling."

We are traveling more than ever and many are heading out on vacations that involve active sports — golf, skiing, fishing, scuba diving, and more. It's fun to try a favorite sport in an exotic new place. Some sports, tennis for example, are very portable and require little beyond tucking a racquet, balls, shoes, and shorts into your suitcase. Others require great packing skills to fit the gear into the car or onto the plane. Check with your airline about size and weight restrictions.

Because these specialized trips may happen infrequently, a packing list that you create and modify each time is a great way to remember details that make a difference. Some people create separate lists for "gear" and "personal items and clothing." The key to success is making a list and checking it often.

Golf

Traveling with golf gear is cumbersome. David first bought a hard-sided golf travel bag with wheels (we called it "the coffin"). It protected his clubs and held my beach umbrella and more. But it was bulky to store, barely fit into our car, and often forced us to rent a larger, more expensive vehicle. Here are some options:

1. Hard-sided golf travel bags are rigid cases with wheels that hold a golf bag with clubs. They don't have extra storage pockets but do provide unmatched protection for the contents, and the large storage cavity holds shoes and golf accessories.

2. Soft-sided golf travel bags are well padded with a rigid base and wheels. This bag zips over both a golf bag and clubs, and has many pockets for golf shoes and gear. The combination of hard shell and soft sides makes this style easier to store and stow in a car.

3. Hybrid golf travel bags do not cover the golf bag — they are the golf bag, but with a detachable hard top that protects the club heads while traveling. This bag type is protective and flexible.

Investing in a quality bag to protect expensive gear is a good idea but think about the logistics. If hauling your clubs is too much trouble, consider renting clubs at your destination but pack your own golf shoes. Playing 18 holes in shoes that don't fit properly could be miserable. Or play with your own clubs without the hassle — call one of the door-to-door luggage services (see page 240) and travel luggage-free!

Necessities

Be sure to pack these items — the ones that are often left behind and are expensive to replace at golf resorts.

- Golf hat or visor
- Golf wind shirt
- Golf umbrella
- Spare golf glove and towel
- Rain gear
- Insect repellent
- Sunscreen of at least 30 SPF

Golf Clothing Tips

If playing golf in hot and humid weather, wear a high-tech, wicking golf shirt. Look for wicking, quick-drying synthetics that feel more comfortable than cotton. (See page 74.)

Wear dark pants or shorts that won't show soil as quickly and you may be able to wear them more than once without laundering. Dark golf socks worn with dark pants won't show grass stains and can be more easily washed by hand. Nancy N. reminds us that dark colors are warmer to wear in hot climates, so packing for a golf vacation in Hawaii may require taking additional pairs of white shorts and socks or doing laundry more often.

Ski/Snowboard

Not only are skis/poles/snowboards plus boots awkward to pack, clothing for these cold weather activities is also bulky. Here are insights about packing to fly to a ski/snowboard vacation.

SMART TRAVEL

Rent skis/snowboard at your destination and pack only your boots, clothes, and off-the-mountain wear. Leslie rents new gear at her destination for every trip – no transportation or home storage hassles, plus she always has the newest equipment.

1. For either skis or snowboards, purchase a well-padded bag that will best protect the contents. Look for a bag with wheels that can be secured with a TSA-approved lock.

2. Try a large duffel on wheels for your second bag — these are a great choice for bulky gear. See pages 119-120 for how to pack a duffel most efficiently. With two wheeled bags you should be able to manage all your belongings through airports and more.

3. Make sure you have adequate insurance to cover the value of this expensive equipment! Either a renter/homeowner policy or added travel insurance is important. See pages 98 and 103 for baggage insurance information.

4. Don't forget your sunscreen. Take a regular-size bottle to use in the morning plus a travel size for your pocket to reapply midday on the mountain.

5. **Ski:** Purchase a double ski bag designed for two pair of skis, even if you will be transporting just one pair. A single bag holds ONLY skis and poles, whereas a double will hold most of your gear.

   First pack your skis and poles into a heavy-duty plastic bag like the type the airlines use for shipping skis. This will keep sharp ski edges from slicing other contents. Place bagged skis and poles into the double ski bag.

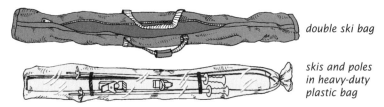

double ski bag

skis and poles in heavy-duty plastic bag

   Next, fill the rest of the ski bag with insulated jackets and pants, sweaters, ski underwear, gloves — anything that isn't breakable. Roll clothing, then tuck inside.

   Pack your boots (if they are easy to replace) in your suitcase and tuck fragile items such as ski goggles into them. Pack around the boots with after ski clothing and toiletries and the rest of your travel and ski gear.

If you really love your ski boots, carry them onto the airplane as I do because I have difficult feet to fit. I can replace everything but my boots if my bags are delayed in transit. Barbara A. transports her boots in a small wheel-aboard bag.

Snowboard: It is possible to check a snowboard in a padded board bag with the bindings attached. To minimize binding damage, experts suggest removing the bindings (just 3-4 screws with a Phillips head screwdriver — pack the driver too) and storing them wrapped in clothing or bubble wrap inside the board bag. Fill the remaining spaces in the bag with boots, rolled clothing, and gear.

Pack high-tech long underwear for skiing or snowboarding. It's so warm that you can often pack less bulky outerwear.

Fishing

Lisa is a world-class sports traveler. From skiing in Chile to bicycling in Tuscany, this woman has done it all! However, her most impressive credentials are in fly fishing. She's been a guide in Idaho and fly fished in northern Russia, Iceland, New Zealand, and Christmas Island — and more. Here are Lisa's best tips for packing for a fishing trip:

1. **Choose duffel bags for both personal things and fishing gear.** When traveling with her husband to fish, they share one large duffel for fishing gear. They each have a personal bag plus a small carry-on with breakables and en route necessities. Fly fishing rods are fragile, so they are always carried on board.

2. **Save and use the large, clear plastic, zipper bags that bedding often comes in** to organize things within an unstructured duffel. These are also available in closet organizer stores and departments. (Two-quart, self-sealing plastic bags are a smaller but less durable substitute.) Lisa packs into these by

category — tee-shirts in one, shorts in another, lingerie in a third, cosmetics and toiletries in the next. (See pages 119-120 for more on packing a duffel.)

3. **Pack items that you can layer; it's the key to staying warm and dry.** Weather can vary tremendously, depending on the locale and the time of year. You may find yourself fishing in a tee-shirt and shorts or wearing many warm layers under chest waders. Here are some of the pieces Lisa packed for a June fishing/camping trip in Montana:

   • Patagonia Synchilla tights for warm sleeping
   • Synchilla pants to wear under waders and in camp
   • Warm socks — pack plenty if laundry options are limited
   • Polyester fleece vest
   • Waterproof Gore-Tex shell jacket
   • Gore-Tex three-quarter length rain jacket with hood

   Lisa's zippered plastic blanket bags were packed daily into a "dry bag" for transporting on the river. Sneakers and river sandals went in first, then the plastic bags with the top one being her toiletries and cosmetics. With last-in-first-out, she could tidy up immediately after reaching camp. Lisa even packs a change of earrings to help her feel "halfway feminine."

4. **Take lots of large and medium-sized plastic garbage bags** so you can bag wet and muddy gear after use. In an ideal world, gear would be dried and cleaned before packing but that is not always possible.

5. **Don't forget sunscreen and industrial strength mosquito repellent.**

Sailing

Jim flies to an exotic port, rents a boat, and bareboat sails for a period of time in the area. His packing suggestions include:

1. **Less is best.** Sailboats have minimal storage so take as little as you can.

2. **Pack in soft-sided duffels** that can be flattened for storing. A structured suitcase will be impossible to store unless you have rented the Queen Mary.

3. **Sunscreen and insect repellent are necessities** so pack a lot. You will always run out days from a store.

4. **Be sure to take a supply of seasick pills, the patch, or wristbands (Sea-Bands).** You never know when you or a passenger might need them.

5. **Shoes with rubber soles are critical for on-board safety.** Sandals for beach use are handy; rubber thongs work for this and for public showers. Leslie recommends "water shoes" or "aqua socks" (rubber soles and a stretchy mesh top) for walking from an anchored boat to shore, and for exploring rocky beaches.

6. **Special sunblock clothing is a great choice** for a sailing vacation. (See page 152.)

7. **Pack some warm layers and rain gear** just in case the sun doesn't shine every minute.

8. **It's smart to pack a couple of "real clothes" outfits** — long pants and a shirt with a collar for men or dresses for women if you think you will be going ashore for nice dinners.

Scuba Diving

Trish and Maurice have traveled all over the world to scuba dive. Since most diving locations are casual places, personal clothing (for Trish and Maurice) consists of shorts and tee-shirts plus lots of swimsuits so a dry one is always available. They use these items to cushion diving equipment and to fill the empty spaces. If Trish needs one dressier outfit, she takes it in her carry-on bag. In addition she shares these tips:

1. **Carry on the irreplaceable or expensive items:** regulator; dive computer; face mask (theirs have prescription lenses).

2. **Never pack scuba equipment in a special diving gear bag.** It's an open invitation to theft in transit. Choose an unmarked, nondescript bag instead.

3. **Choose structured luggage for the best protection for your gear.** Trish and Maurice each take a 28" hard-sided bag that holds diving gear and personal clothing, plus a carry-on with the above listed items and things they'll need during the flight.

CHAPTER 18

Packing for Kids

Kids are cool! Find ways to involve them in the travel planning.

Traveling with kids takes more planning, but the rewards are tremendous. Showing your children a world larger than their hometown is a great investment in their education. History and geography become real when kids watch the blacksmith at work in Williamsburg, Virginia, or see the awesome power of the river in the Amazon.

Since children of varying ages have such different needs, read through this chapter and highlight only what is pertinent to your family for the trip at hand.

Get Your Kids Involved!

1. **Include your children in travel decision making, planning, and preparation.** Anticipation is half the fun. Use books, videos, even music tapes to help them visualize your destination. Plan your route with an atlas or globe to show them where in the world they're going. Then, as you travel, let them mark your route each day so they can see where they've been and where you're headed.

2. **Teach packing skills.** Have your children create their own packing lists and pack their own bags. Give guidelines for the amount of clothing needed and when their clothing favorites need to be clean and ready to pack. Double-check their packed bags to make sure that live pets are not included and that underwear is!

3. **Help them pack into fewer, larger bags when baggage must be checked** so there will be less chance of a small bag being lost or left behind. Otherwise, have each child pack their own bag and make sure you do a bag count at every unpacking stop. Each child should have a backpack for day use, perfect for an airline, bus, or train carry-on. Fill it with books, toys, games and other items that will be used on board. Include snacks, juice boxes, and a sweater or jacket. The pack will also come in handy for day excursions en route.

Clothes to Go for Kids

1. **Help children select favorite clothing items that are versatile, easy-care, and comfortable to wear.** Knits are a good choice, plus they can be rolled for quick packing and won't wrinkle easily. Darker colors and prints hide dirt and stains, white and light colors are magnets for spots.

2. **Show kids how to pack into self-sealing plastic bags —** lots of them in various sizes. Pack each daily outfit — underwear, socks, top and bottom — into its own plastic bag; at the end of the day, the dirty clothes go back into the same bag. Or, sort the dirty clothes by laundry load into larger bags and save the clean daily bags for repacking daily outfits after a laundry stop.

SMART TRAVEL Tip

Stack a daily outfit — top, pants, underwear, socks — and roll all at once to keep things together. The roll can be placed in plastic bag, or not as you choose. See page 108 for rolling tips.

3. **Pack for layering to accommodate weather;** for example, sweater + windbreaker = warm jacket. Fleece layers pack small, are easy-care and very warm. Include one off-season item for everyone — long pants in summer or shorts for spring and fall. Should the weather change, you'll all be covered — comfortably.

4. **Pack a favorite stuffed animal, blanket, and pillow** to help a child sleep better in new and strange environments. Sleep masks and ear plugs for each family member are also helpful.

Take The Right Kid Equipment

The right equipment is essential for traveling with kids — for their safety as well as their comfort *and* yours. Please be considerate of other airline passengers and do not attempt to carry-on all of the following pieces at one time!

- Airlines suggest kids up to 40 pounds fly in a car seat. To guarantee a seat for the car seat you must often pay full fare; however, children under two fly free if they are held on a parent's lap. The choice is yours: If the flight is not full there may be room for the car seat; if full, put the seat in the overhead bin or gate-check it. A new option is the CARES™ — "child aviation restraint system" — a seatbelt that attaches to the back of the airplane seat and augments the regular seat belt. It weighs only one pound and fits into a purse or pocket, and adapts the aircraft seat belt to fit children from 22 to 44 pounds (www.kidsflysafe.com).

- A lightweight, collapsible umbrella stroller can be a lifesaver for tired parents and kids. Taking your own will save hours of standing in the stroller rental line. Some museums and attractions do not allow them so always call ahead to verify. Umbrella strollers are generally an acceptable airline carry-on piece, or they can be gate checked.

- Backpack-style child carriers are an advantage on rough terrain or in crowds where a stroller is awkward. These are appropriate for children from about 6 months to 3 years or up to 40 pounds in weight. You can place a backpack carrier in a large airline plastic bag and check it curbside, or use it to carry your child to the boarding area and then gate-check it. Liesje feels the backpack carrier is too bulky to handle for air travel and prefers a stroller for her daughter instead.

SMART TRAVEL *Gadget*

The Piggyback Stroller by Manten is small and lightweight and converts to a backpack. The Piggyback weighs 5 pounds and holds a child of 6 months to 2 years old, or up to 33 pounds. Check with your local retailer or www.gobabies.com. Also available is the Convertible Carrier by Kelty (www.kelty.com).

- Liesje disassembled a baby bouncer and packed it in her suitcase. Baby Delaney happily bounced away poolside and in their hotel room.

- Renting kids gear at your destination is getting easier; check with www.babysaway.com for US locations. Popular parenting website www.babiestravellite.com does not rent baby equipment but they provide a list of baby equipment rental agencies for most major cities worldwide.

TRAVELING WITH INFANTS

"Start then while they are young" says Pati, whose daughter had a frequent flyer number issued at birth. "Getting used to traveling early is best for baby and parents." Infants are quite portable, even though they require lots of gear.

1. Prevent ear problems. We know to swallow to balance ear pressure on take-off and landing; babies need to do the same. Provide a bottle or breast feed to make them swallow. A pacifier helps too. Doctors also recommend filtered earplugs www.cirrushealthcare.com/EarPlanes) for children over one year old. These slowly equalize the pressure against the eardrum during takeoff and landing.

2. Plan for at least two changes of clothing for the baby and one for yourself and lots of extra diapers, plus extra clean-up supplies and extra clean blankets, even for a short flight or car trip. You don't have to pack enough diapers for the entire trip—have diapers, formula, and all other baby supplies delivered to your vacation destination (www.babiestravellite.com).

3. Take enough warm clothing (extra blankets, a hat and sweater). The temperature on public transportation is often frigid.

4. Take extra plastic bottles of juice or milk and understand that flight attendants often do not have time to warm bottles on short flights. New security regulations allow medications, baby formula and food, breast milk, and juice in reasonable quantities and are not required to be placed in the "3-1-1 zip-top bag." Declare these items for inspection at the checkpoint.

5. Carry baby in a soft infant carrier to keep your hands free for other tasks. Unlike a backpack-style carrier with a frame, soft carriers pack small.

Travel Safety for Kids

You want your children to feel as safe on the road as they do in their home. Be sure to read through this list before you leave home, so you'll have the things you need to provide a safe environment wherever your travels take you.

1. **Child-proof a hotel room** just as you would your home. Travel with your own safety plugs for electrical outlets if you have toddlers and use any other at-home precautions necessary.

2. **Keep any medications locked in a suitcase** and away from curious little ones — like a locked medicine chest at home.

3. **Consider using a wrist leash or harness for your toddler** when you are in crowded areas. There is nothing more frightening than losing sight of your child, even for a moment — and just think how frightened your child will be if they lose you!

4. **Make sure each child has identification on them** in the form of an ID bracelet, a dog-tag-style necklace, a tag sewn into their clothing, or a note tucked into a pocket, a pack, or purse. For local information, tuck a business card with the name and address of your hotel in a pocket. If you should get separated, someone will know where to call.

5. **Put kids' names inside clothing,** *not* on the outside. Avoid monogrammed or printed names on outer clothing. Children assume when a stranger calls them by name that the person is a friend.

6. **Be sure your hands are free to hold onto your children,** especially when walking in crowded areas. Wearing a backpack instead of carrying a purse or tote bag makes this easier. Whatever you're doing, walk with your children in front of you where you can see them.

7. **Include a current, clear, front-view photo of your children with your valuable travel documents.** Write a list of distinguishing marks for each child on the back of the photo for easy identification.

8. **Use the "buddy system."** A child should always have a "buddy" — a parent, an adult friend, another child, a brother or sister — to go anywhere; that includes going on the elevator to the hotel lobby, to the bathroom in any public facility, or to buy a soft drink down the hall.

WRITTEN PARENTAL PERMISSION

PAY ATTENTION TO THIS!

If your child is traveling internationally with one parent, a relative, or a friend, that person is required to present a notarized letter of permission from the child's other parent or parents in order to board an aircraft. **Travel will be denied without this document.** This is also true when driving across a US border to Mexico or Canada. Unfortunately, too many children have been kidnapped and taken out of the country by a parent disputing custody.

Keep Your Kids Healthy On the Road

It's bad enough to be sick at home, but nothing can destroy a trip faster than an illness or an accident. Add the disappointment of reaching the destination and having to stay in bed while everyone else has fun and you have a very unhappy child and parents.

1. **Carry your pediatrician's phone and fax number** when traveling. A quick phone call to a physician who knows your child can save a stop at an emergency room or a visit to a strange doctor's office.

2. **Pack and use lots of sunscreen** and be sure to reapply after swimming or routinely every couple of hours. Teach your kids to wear wide-brimmed hats that cover their faces and ears, not just baseball caps. Babies should not be in the sun at all.

3. **Take insect repellent formulated for children** — a must in most areas. The CDC recommends applying repellent to your own hands and then rubbing it onto the child, avoiding the eyes and mouth. Do not apply repellent to children's hands as they tend to put their hands in their mouths. Wash off repellent after returning indoors.

4. **Use antibacterial hand cleaners and individually wrapped antibacterial moist towelettes** — one of the century's best sanitary inventions. Older children should carry their own in their packs.

5. **Teach your children to drink only bottled water and to use it when brushing their teeth, too,** when traveling where water quality may be questionable. Teach them not to swallow water in the tub, shower, or swimming pool. At your destination, purchase large containers of bottled water (or travel with your own purifying equipment) and refill everyone's personal water bottle frequently. Canned or bottled soft drinks that you open and *drink through a straw* and *without ice* are OK too. See page 207 for more information on water quality and safety.

6. **Pack a Children's Traveling Medicine Chest. Include:**

   - Phone and fax numbers for your pediatrician and any other regular physicians

   - An adequate supply of any prescription medications, plus written copies of the prescription in a carry-on bag

   - Digital thermometer (mercury thermometers may be banned on international flights)

   - Children's-strength aspirin, acetaminophen, or ibuprofen as recommended by your doctor

   - Motion sickness medication (ask your doctor)

   - Antihistamine (liquid for small children) to combat chronic allergies and possible allergic reactions

   - Decongestant for colds and sinus congestion

   - Anti-diarrhea medication (ask your doctor)

   - Insect repellent and anti-sting or itch-relief product such as calamine lotion or cortisone cream

   - Supplies for cuts and scrapes — kids' Band-Aids®, gauze, bandages, adhesive tape, first aid cream, antibacterial soap, and antibacterial ointment

Necessities

Toys, food, and clean-up items are all part of life with kids — and you'll need them on the road, too. Here are some things moms suggest to make the trip with kids a little more carefree.

1. Favorite toys supply a sense of security. New toys purchased for the trip, portioned out as the surprise of the day or hour, can entertain during long and boring travel segments. Gift wrapping already favorite toys adds newness and a sense of adventure at minimal expense.

2. Hungry children and formal mealtimes may not coincide. Bridget says "Always plan for the unexpected and carry food and drinks with you." Juice boxes and water bottles are a must. Each child should carry a personal water bottle in their backpack every day. This helps to avoid the "too much sugar from soft drinks" syndrome, while still getting enough liquid to ward off constipation. Nutritious and portable snacks such as the following are all good choices:

   - apples
   - baby carrots
   - bananas
   - cereal
   - crackers
   - granola bars
   - grapes
   - raisins

3. Having your own healthy food available can be as simple as packing the family cooler in the car or purchasing an inexpensive cooler at your destination. I like a small, soft, insulated cooler bag that folds flat in my luggage. I fill self-sealing plastic bags with ice cubes for daily use. Liz purchased a large collapsible cooler; she packs it in her checked suitcase to use when traveling in a rental car.

4. Picnic supplies are a travel lifesaver and money saver on the road. With a quick stop at the grocery store and the following items in your travel gear, you can prepare an inexpensive picnic breakfast in your room or a lunch for the park, thus avoiding the restaurant hassles that are often common when dining out with children:

   - Blanket or space blanket for "on-the-ground" picnics
   - Paper or plastic plates and bowls
   - Paper towels or napkins
   - Plastic tablecloth (or yesterday's newspaper)
   - Plastic utensils, including spoons for cereal
   - Pocket or Swiss army knife (pack in checked bags only) or a can opener

5. Pack plenty of clean-up materials: tissues and paper towels (I always have a roll in the car for spills and cleaning the windshield); damp paper towels in a self-sealing plastic bag; individually wrapped moist towelettes; antibacterial hand cleaner; Travel Towls (see page 156) cut into quarters, dampened, and placed in a self-sealing plastic bag.

6. A night light will help everyone navigate in a strange hotel room — and helps to keep the monsters at bay. These are also available for international travel.

7. Take along a separate luggage cart, even if your luggage has built-in wheels. Wheelies are great for hauling your cooler to the beach, the family's carry-on luggage through an airport, or your gear between the car and the motel room.

Family Air Travel Tips

Keep air travel fun by planning ahead. Here are some tips to help ensure that flying with your family is worry free and enjoyable so you enjoy the trip of your dreams rather than a travel nightmare.

1. **Plan flights carefully.** Ask your travel agent which flights have the best on-time record, which are non-stops, which are the least crowded, and which days are less hectic than others. Spend more to fly on a slower day, rather than buying the cheapest ticket and finding the flight/airport overcrowded.

2. **Consider morning flights (after the 6-7 am crunch).** They are a good choice because there are generally other flight options if your morning flight is delayed or canceled.

3. **Choose non-stop flights to minimize potential delays.** It's worth an extra cost. Direct flights with a stop but no change of planes increase the possibility of delays with every stop, but are better than changing planes. If you must change planes, the potential for delays increases dramatically.

4. **Ask if food is served on the flight**. If nothing is available, pack food for your family. Avoid the horror of a two-hour delay onboard an aircraft with no food. Liquids must be purchased inside the airport secure area. Granola bars, crackers, bananas, and apples travel well. Antibacterial hand cleaner and moist towelettes are also must-pack items for family travel.

Family Packing List

Use the Children's Traveling Medicine Chest (page 173), and Necessities lists (pages 174-175), plus the lists here that apply to you to create your own basic kid-travel packing list. Add clothing and travel items that apply to your family. Be specific: List each clothing item for each person so you have a checklist to make sure something isn't left under the bed or at the self-service laundry.

Packing List for Kids

• Favorite comfortable clothes plus warm layers

• Self-sealing plastic bags

• Favorite stuffed animal, blanket, and pillow

• Car seat or CARES (see page 169)

• Collapsible umbrella stroller

• Backpack-style child carrier

• Baby bouncer

• Soft fabric infant carrier

• Extra clothing changes for en route

• Childproofing equipment for hotel room

• Wrist leash or harness

• Identification for each child to wear or carry

• Photo of each child or group photo with ID information on back

• Day pack for parents

• Notarized letter authorizing parent or another adult to travel with a child

• Pediatrician's phone and fax number

• Sunscreen and hats

• Insect repellent

• Water bottles

• Antibacterial hand cleaner or moist towelettes

Packing List for Babies

Liesje is a busy working mom with two children, a very demanding career, and (thank goodness!) a helpful husband. As of this writing, she has two little ones — McKenna is 3 and Delaney is 6 months. She has traveled with them a lot so she knows what she is talking about! Liesje created this list from her kid-travel experiences. Modify it as necessary to meet your needs.

- Diapers

- Plastic bags (lots!) for dirty diapers

- Changing pad

- Diaper wipes

- Diaper rash medicine

- Sunscreen

- Bottles

- Sippy cup

- Bibs

- Baby spoon

- Insulated bag for milk

- Snacks

- Toys

- Extra clean clothes

- Hat, booties, sweater, blanket

- Portable crib and crib sheet

- Car seat

- Soft infant carrier, front-pack style

Part IV:

TRAVEL SAFELY IN COMFORT & GOOD HEALTH

To be healthy and happy while away requires planning.

Maximize fun and minimize problems by heeding these chapters.

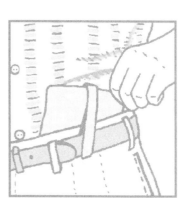

CHAPTER 19

Before You Leave Home

Checklists relieve stress without prescription drugs!

Use this checklist before you leave to ensure peace of mind while traveling. The goal is to leave your home looking like someone is there. Create your own list of tasks that pertain to your home and lifestyle so that you don't forget the details in the crunch of leaving.

Ten Things to Do Before You Go

❏ 1. **Ask a relative, trusted friend, or neighbor to keep an eye on your home.** They should have a key and your burglar alarm codes and instructions in case of an emergency. Ask them to pick up unexpected deliveries and remove anything that announces to the passerby that you aren't home.

❏ 2. **Leave a detailed itinerary** with your house watcher that includes destination phone numbers so you can be reached in an emergency.

❏ 3. **Stop the newspaper for long trips.** If delivery is not stopped as ordered, your watchful friend should pick up the paper and notify the carrier.

❏ 4. **Have your mail held at the post office for long trips,** to be picked up upon your return. If you are delayed and the post office delivers two week's worth of mail, you will have a breach of security and a mess to clean up.

❏ 5. **Ask your house watcher to pick up your newspapers and mail** if your trip is just for a couple of days.

❏ 6. **Arrange for outdoor maintenance.** Ask someone to water your lawn and plants and to mow the grass. In winter, having someone shovel your walk and driveway will keep up appearances that "someone is home."

❏ 7. **Pay your bills.**

❏ 8. **Put lights and a radio on timers** with varying on-and-off times. A casual burglar will not break into a house with lights on and sounds inside.

❏ 9. **Arrange to have the trash put out** and cans replaced after pick-up.

❏ 10. **Make arrangements for pet care** as far in advance as possible. You may find the cost of an in-home pet-sitter who will also house-sit is comparable to boarding your pet. (Roz feels cats do better left in their own environment with a sitter.) Ask for references and make sure sitters are licensed, bonded, and insured. The sitter should have your itinerary and a detailed list of pet care and home care tasks that you expect to be performed. They should take care of all the items for your house watcher as listed above.

CHAPTER 20

Travel In Comfort

Fatigue is not your friend.
Find ways to stay rested and happy.

For a long trip the most important thing to me is to be comfortable, yet I still want to be attractively dressed. I travel in something I can wear for business or for touring the next day if my luggage and I don't connect as planned. I have nightmares of attending business meetings in a jogging suit and so have never traveled that casually. I plan my travel outfit as part of my overall wardrobe so I can wear the pieces throughout the trip.

Choose Comfortable Clothing For Long Trips

As you plan your travel wardrobe, be sure to think about what you will wear in transit. Constricting clothing is a poor choice for long periods in planes, trains, buses, and automobiles. The list below is based on years of travel experience.

1. **Loose waistlines** are best for all modes of travel. The altitude and air pressure in flight cause swelling of the extremities and bloating. Give yourself plenty of expansion room by wearing an elastic-waist pants or skirt, or a waistline with plenty of possible adjustments. See page 42 for some ideas. I find jeans to be the least comfortable choice, unless they have Lycra added to give them comfort stretch. Avoid wide belts or large belt buckles that will cut into your middle when seated.

2. **Separate tops and bottoms** are comfortable and are easy to maneuver in the world's smallest bathrooms — on airplanes and buses. *Never travel in a jumpsuit;* it is almost impossible to deal with in tight quarters!

3. **Soft breathable knits in roomy styles** are the most comfortable things to wear. This does not mean sweats. One of my favorites is a cotton knit dress with an elastic waist. Some other comfortable yet appropriate travel pieces are shown on the next page.

4. **Comfortable flat shoes and a pair of warm socks** (in your carry-on in case you need them) are essential. After departure,

loosen your shoes or take them off and slip on the socks. Your feet will stay warm and comfortable for the duration of the trip. You will have to put your shoes on to disembark, so shoes should be roomy — I guarantee your feet will swell! Tucking a small shoe horn into your carry-on will help. Avoid wearing close-fitting boots on long trips — they are bad for circulation.

5. **For women, wear your loosest and most comfortable bra.** If there is any way you can avoid wearing one and wear a camisole instead, I recommend it. Also, underwire bras are detected in airport security screening and may trigger a wand search or a hand pat-down.

6. **For men, David suggests wearing your roomiest, least binding pair of undershorts.**

7. **A warm layer such as a sweater, shawl, or windbreaker** in your carry-on bag is essential, even for summer travel. Travel conveyances and terminals are often over air-conditioned.

8. **Pack a change of underwear, a clean top, and your medications, cosmetics and toiletries in your carry-on bag** (3 ounces [100ml] or less in your "3-1-1- zip-top bag). If I am headed to a beach, I pack a swimsuit. If my luggage is delayed, I have something clean to wear. If it is delayed for more than one day, I go shopping.

Comfortable Travel Clothes

In-Transit Creature Comforts

Every passenger has a different idea of what makes traveling comfortable. Here are some suggestions for the trip:

1. **Consider not wearing make-up when on a long flight.** Going "faceless" makes it easy to reapply moisturizer frequently and use a water spritzer. Just prior to arrival or in the airport, slip into the bathroom and apply make-up.

2. **Apply lip balm and hand lotion often** to help combat dry skin.

3. **Pack toothpaste and a travel toothbrush in your carry-on.** A clean mouth can be a real pick-me-up in the wee hours of the morning when you are ready to land in a foreign country!

4. **Take plenty of water** (in addition to what may be served), healthy snacks, breath mints, tissues, and antibacterial towelettes or hand cleaner.

5. **Choose a window seat if you want to sleep** undisturbed by others who need to get up and down during the trip. Choose an aisle seat if you want to walk and stretch regularly or need to use the bathroom frequently.

6. **Request a pillow, blanket, and magazines as soon as you board.** These amenities go fast. If you are not cold, the blanket can be rolled up and placed behind the small of your back for a lumbar support with the pillow supporting your neck and head. If you are short, prop up your feet with another pillow or blanket or use your carry-on bag to relieve pressure on the backs of your legs during flight.

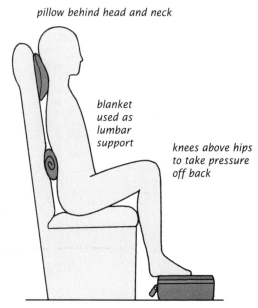

pillow behind head and neck

blanket used as lumbar support

knees above hips to take pressure off back

feet elevated on carry-on bag, pillows, or blanket

SMART TRAVEL *Gadget*

Here are some gadgets illustrated below that pack small but deliver big comfort, especially on a long flight. All are available in travel and luggage shops and from catalog and online travel merchants.

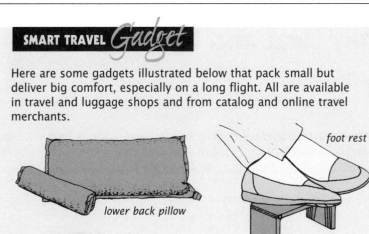

foot rest

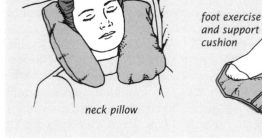

lower back pillow

foot exercise and support cushion

neck pillow

7. **Take a paperback book or magazines** (which are lighter than books and disposable). You may want your portable CD or DVD player (putting on earphones is a sure way to silence a chatty seatmate). Books on tape or CD or MP3 player are my favorite; they make long car trips pass in a flash. Playing cards, portable games, and crossword puzzles all help while away long traveling sessions.

8. **Noise-canceling headphones** almost completely eliminate the drone of aircraft engines and background noise so you arrive feeling less exhausted from sound overload from the flight. In addition, they improve the quality of in-flight audio. Prices range from inexpensive to extravagant, and only your ears can determine what is comfortable and sounds terrific to you. They are available at electronic and travel retailers everywhere.

9. **Pack a sleep mask and earplugs.** These can help even the worst insomniac sleep while traveling and they're great in hotels, too.

CHAPTER 21

Stay Neat and Clean

Easy does it. Don't make work out of staying clean.

The secret to traveling light is taking fewer things and wearing each piece more often. That makes clothes care very important. You can send things to the hotel laundry if you have enough time and are willing to pay a lot for the service, but here is how to do it yourself with the least fuss.

First, Unpack

Unpack and hang your clothes immediately after checking into your room if at all possible. Shake each item well and hang to air out and shed packing wrinkles. If you packed in a humid locale, you will find more wrinkling than if you packed in a dry climate. If wrinkles don't fall out overnight, hang the items in the bathroom while you take a steamy shower. If stubborn wrinkles still remain, barely moisten a washcloth and lightly brush the wrinkles to ease them away, then blow with a hair dryer. (Don't do this to a silk blouse or anything that water spots.) Give damp clothes time to dry before wearing.

SMART TRAVEL *Tip*

Karen "presses" wrinkles away in scarves and ties and other soft fabrics by running the item over a heated light bulb. Be sure to wipe the bulb free of dust first!

SMART TRAVEL *Gadget*

Pack "Wrinkle Free™," a fabric relaxant in a can that sprays wrinkles away. It also eliminates static cling but takes up less space and weighs less than a steamer or travel iron, Buy the smaller three-ounce can, available from travel and luggage stores. Faultless® Wrinkle Remover is a similar product.

WHAT ABOUT TRAVEL IRONS AND STEAMERS?

If you have selected travel-friendly fabrics and packed to minimize wrinkles, you won't need an iron or a steamer. Even if you travel with things that wrinkle, you may not need to pack an iron. In-room irons and ironing boards are becoming a standard, even in budget motel chains. To find out how your room is equipped, call your motel/hotel. If you feel you need to pack your own iron or steamer, you'll find these widely available wherever small electrical appliances are sold. For an ironing board, simply turn back the covers and press on the bottom sheet of the bed.

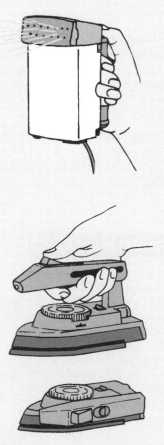

A steamer is generally lighter weight but bulkier than a travel iron. It creates steam to soften wrinkles and smooth fabrics but it does not have a hot sole plate so you can't crease a pair of pants with one. Look for a steamer that uses regular tap water; dual voltage plus adaptor plugs are important for international travel.

A travel iron is a smaller version of a home iron and many have handles that fold flat to save space. Look for both steam- and dry-iron features. The more steam vents the better as the iron will press faster. A non-stick sole plate is a real plus and dual voltage plus adaptor plugs are important for international travel. Lightweight is the most important feature.

Be Tidy!

Your mother was right. If you hang your clothes carefully when you take them off, the wrinkles *will* hang out. Pack a clip-type hanger plus spot remover and a lint brush or roller or a roll of masking tape to remove lint.

1. **Hang your pants on a clip-type hanger from the cuffs or hem,** carefully lining up the creases. Leaving your belt in the belt loops adds weight to help the wrinkles hang out.

2. **When needed, use a spot remover as soon as possible.** (See page 188 for product recommendations.)

3. **Hang your jacket on an appropriate hanger, outside the closet,** so it can air for the next wearing. Use a lint brush or lint roller if needed.

4. **Hang your shirt/blouse if it can be worn another day.** Roz suggests turning the item inside out for the best airing. If not wearable, put it back in the bottom of your suitcase or in your dirty laundry pocket so it is already packed.

SMART TRAVEL *Item*

Underarm shields for both men and women, available in fabric stores, make it possible to wear a shirt or dress more than once before cleaning or washing. The disposable type is most convenient for travel. (www.kleinertsshields.com)

SMART TRAVEL

Everyone needs a small sewing kit for emergency repairs. Some hotels provide handy little kits with the complimentary shampoo; tuck one of these into your suitcase. You can also find small sewing kits in travel shops and fabric stores. I like to carry a small pair of folding scissors with me, too.

Plan for Hand Laundry

Here are the hand laundry supplies I pack for trips of a week or more in length. Most are available at travel and luggage stores, department, drug, supermarket, or discount stores. With the exception of the clip-type hangers, these laundry supplies fit into a quart-size, self-sealing plastic bag that takes no more space than a pair of underwear. I refill supplies when I get home and keep them in the suitcase, ready for the next trip.

1. **Soap.** Take a small bottle of liquid dishwashing detergent from home, preferably a product that can be used in both hot and cold water. Sporting goods departments sell biodegradable soap for back-country use. Steve suggests a chunk of Fels Naptha bar soap stored in a film canister. Woolite® is available in handy single-use foil packets. If I am traveling luxuriously, I use the shampoo samples provided by the hotel.

2. **Flat rubber sink stopper.** Ever since I lost a contact lens down a loose sink drain in Paris, I have carried one of these. If the sink won't hold water, how can you wash your socks? Bathtub users also take note.

3. **Clothesline.** The Flexo-line holds clothes without clothespins.

4. **Inflatable hangers.** These lightweight, blow-up, plastic hangers help air circulation so clothes dry faster. June S. recommends taking two.

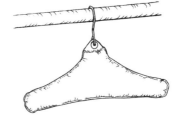

5. **Hanging clothespins.** These

handy clips (take two along) hang from places where a clothesline won't work. I have dried pantyhose on a hanging clip hung on a lampshade so the heat of the lamp would speed drying. You can also use them to clip together draperies that don't quite black out the light.

6. **Clip-type hangers.** Hotels never seem to have enough of these and often they have the kind you cannot take off the rod to hang in the bathroom if you need to steam something. Take two of your own to use for eliminating packing wrinkles and for laundry drying as well as for hanging clothing.

7. **Spot and stain remover.** Treat stains as soon as possible to prevent them from setting. Janie® Spot Cleaner and Stain Eraser™ are two small wonders that travel well and handle most stains. I also like Shout® Wipes towelettes and the Tide to Go® laundry "pen".

Basin Laundry Basics

1. Fill the bathroom basin with warm water and add a small amount of liquid detergent. Apply extra detergent to spots, underarms, and collar on the dry garment — and any other place that needs extra attention — and rub gently. If you get the item wet first, spots are harder to find. Roxanne suggests using an old toothbrush to gently brush spots.

2. Rinse at least twice in warm water. Leftover soap residue can cause skin irritations in hot and humid weather.

3. For items that may wrinkle: Squeeze gently while washing and rinsing; wringing makes deep wrinkles. Hang the item on an inflatable hanger or clip-type hanger, buttoning or zipping as needed, and allow to drip dry over the tub or in the shower.

For items that will not wrinkle: Wring out as much water as possible, then flatten out on a towel and roll to remove remaining water. Hang to dry.

SMART TRAVEL

The bathroom is generally the room with the poorest circulation. To speed up drying time, hang your laundry where the air is — from a door jam, a light fixture in the center of the room, or on the back of a chair in front of the air conditioner or window. Connect the Flexo-line between pieces of furniture. Use a hair dryer later to dry damp areas or to remove wrinkles.

Packing Dirty Clothes

Dirty clothes are a fact of life on the road just as they are at home. But, you won't have a laundry basket or hamper in hotel room, so you'll need a plan for how you will pack them as you go.

1. **Keep dirty clothes separate from clean items.** Place small soiled items in a plastic bag or plastic-lined suitcase pocket.

2. **Place larger soiled items flat in the bottom of your bag and cover with a plastic cleaner's bag.** Repacking to go home will be a snap since most things will already be in the bag.

3. **Pack a small duffel in your suitcase to hold dirty clothes and fill it as you travel.** Refill your suitcase with new shopping treasures and check your dirty laundry in the duffel. This bag can also be used to carry things to and from the self-service laundry en route.

4. **Pack dirty clothes as carefully as you packed your clean clothes.** Dirties always seem to take up more room than clean things — or so it seems.

SMART TRAVEL *Gadget*

Compression bags create up to 75% more space by removing the air from your clothes. Unfortunately, most things wrinkle when the air is compressed away. My favorite use for these is for dirty clothes when wrinkles don't matter. (See page 106 for illustration and sources.)

5. **Look for laundry facilities in your motel/hotel for extended trips and when traveling with children.** Many provide coin-operated machines for guest use. If not, check out the Yellow Pages or ask at your hotel desk. Buying supplies at the laundry is convenient but expensive. Packing a few dryer sheets as well as measured amounts of detergent in self-sealing plastic bags is certainly cheaper and worth the effort if you have room in your luggage.

CHAPTER 22

Worthwhile Travel Gadgets

Don't underestimate — a great gadget can save your sanity!

There is an abundance of travel gadgets available — some of them are essential and some are marginally useful. Before you buy, ask yourself if this product is really going to make your life easier or better. Many, in my opinion, are not worth their space or weight. Read, evaluate, and decide which ones fit your travel styles.

Many useful travel aids have been listed throughout this book with the "Smart Travel Gadget" logo. Your travel store or luggage shop should have a good selection of travel items, including electrical products. Also look for them in department, discount, drug, and sporting goods stores, travel stores, online, and in catalogs.

Electric Gadgets

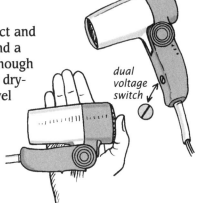

dual
voltage
switch

- **Hair dryer.** Mine is very compact and lightweight, has dual voltage and a collapsible handle. I love it. Although many places I stay provide hair dryers, I prefer my own. Some travel hair dryers are really under powered — look for at least 800 watts of power or your hair will never dry.

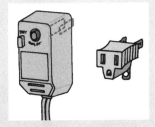

SMART TRAVEL *tip*

By law, American manufacturers must now use Ground Fault Circuit Interrupter (GFCI) plugs on all hair dryers. This plug is a large rectangular box and will not fit into some space-restricted electrical outlets. If you already own or buy a new hair dryer with this type of plug, buy a "grounding adaptor" for about $1.00 in the hardware store, a plug adaptor for international travel (see page 194), or pack an extension cord.

SMART TRAVEL

It's a good idea to pack an extension cord when traveling with electrical products. Hotel room outlets are guaranteed to be at least six feet from where you need one. When sharing a bathroom, I sometimes dry my hair in the bedroom — a difficult task without an extension cord.

- **Curling iron.** For years this was a necessity for me but no longer. Now I have a blow-dry hairdo — perfect for travel! Look for a compact, dual-voltage electric curling iron that retracts for packing.

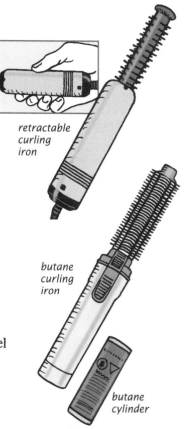

retractable curling iron

Lisa uses a butane-powered curling iron on camping trips — no electricity needed. Airlines consider butane to be a hazardous material but allow one butane cylinder inside a curling iron to be packed in checked baggage, not in carry-on.

butane curling iron

- **Hot rollers.** These are available in travel versions. 10-roller and 5-roller sets are available in travel shops and departments.

butane cylinder

SMART TRAVEL

Lynn packs her curling iron and round curling brush in cardboard tubes to prevent heat damage and breakage.

- **Coffee gear.** I need an early-morning jolt in my room just to get to the nearest coffee shop. I use an immersion coil with a lightweight, heat-tolerant plastic mug. Instant coffee and "plastic" cream go with me in doubled, self-sealing plastic bags. This is worth every inch of space for my morning sanity and is also handy for herbal tea, hot chocolate, instant soups, and more.

immersion coil

Pati insists on freshly ground coffee, not just instant, and in the past traveled with beans and a grinder! Now she buys ground coffee and packs her drip filter beverage maker. She says it's well worth the space.

- **Iron or steamer.** See page 185.

beverage maker

Choosing Electrical Travel Gadgets

Make sure you purchase items that won't add unnecessary weight and will provide the service you need wherever you travel. Look for these features:

1. **Lightweight.** Those ounces really add up quickly. If two products are similar, always choose the lighter one.

2. **Compact.** Items with folding handles, that are smaller in size, and that collapse or nest together, take up less precious space.

3. **Dual voltage.** This is a great option because you never know when an international travel opportunity may present itself. Dual voltage means that the appliance will work in the United States where electrical current is 110 volts, and with a flip of a special switch, will also work at 220 volts — what most of the rest of the world uses.

WHAT ABOUT INTERNATIONAL ELECTRICITY?

In the United States, electricity operates at 110 volt (V) Alternating Current (AC), while most of the rest of the world operates on 220V AC. That is twice as many volts as we use. (These numbers are actually a range from 110 volts up to 125 volts and 220 volts up to 250 volts.) If you plug your 110V hair dryer into a 220V outlet, the motor runs twice as fast as it was built to go. You will probably burn up your hair dryer, perhaps the outlet, and possibly the hotel!

To avoid problems, do the following to be able to use your electrical appliances:

1. **Buy a dual voltage appliance** that changes from 110V to 220V with the flip of a switch, then remember to flip that switch before using.

2. **Buy a voltage converter** for your 110V appliances. A converter takes 220V electricity and cuts the number of volts flowing to your appliance in half. Plug your appliance into the converter, then plug the converter into the outlet.

3. **Buy plug adaptors.** There are at least eleven different non-grounded and ten grounded socket shapes in the world, including the two we use in the US. Even if you purchase a dual-voltage appliance or a voltage converter, you will still not be able to plug in without adaptors.

   Check with a good travel or luggage store to find out which plug adaptors you need for your trip. Some sources offer sets of the most commonly used adaptors.

4 most common plug adaptors

4. **You may still need to be creative to actually plug in.**
Leslie found that her hair dryer would not work in Mexico
because it had a polarized plug (one fat and
one skinny prong) and her hotel had non-
polarized (two skinny prongs) outlets. An
adaptor is available for this purpose and it
makes sense to have one with you at all times.
There are older hotels and charming bed and breakfasts
that may still have this configuration.

The same situation can occur with recessed wall outlets
around the world. An additional extender may be required
for your adaptor to reach the socket.

If you have never traveled internationally, this may sound
very confusing. It's a good example of the huge differences
that still exist, even though our world seems to be getting
smaller. Not every country does it like we do.

5. **Some additional considerations include:**

- American appliances such as hair dryers operate on 60
  cycles per second or "hertz" while international electric
  systems use 50 cycles or hertz (often shown as "Hz"). This
  means you may notice a slowdown in the motor and it may
  take you longer to dry your hair but it will not do any damage to the appliance.

- Some international hotels have 110V outlets marked "For
  Shavers Only." These will work for low wattage items such
  as electric shavers or toothbrushes. Do not use with higher
  wattage appliances such as a hair dryer.

- Some cruise ships have 220V electrical current; check with
  your travel agent or cruise line to see if you need dual voltage appliances or a converter. Some ships also provide hair
  dryers or converters in each stateroom.

- Converters adapt AC current only; they will not work with
  Direct Current (DC) — the type provided by batteries and
  found on some boats and planes.

- Always check the type of current before plugging in.

And if you think all this is confusing, try telephone and
modem connections!

For up-to-date international electrical and telephone
information, view Steve Kropla's "Help for World Travelers"
(www.kropla.com).

Some Favorite Travel Items

Look for these in travel and luggage stores, catalogs, and online.

- **Travel ID holder.** Use a convenient ID holder to have your identification safe and ready without opening your wallet at every airport security checkpoint. Look for one that fits comfortably around your neck and holds a passport for international travel or a driver's license for domestic travel. It should also have a place to hold your boarding pass.

- **Small, lightweight, collapsible umbrella.** I like one that fits into my coat pocket or little travel purse. Look for a handle that is comfortable to hold, one that is easy to open and close, lightweight (between 5-7 ounces), and has an open canopy of at least 38".

- **Disposable plastic rain poncho.** This small, folded square opens into a full-sized poncho with a hood; it's perfect for storing in the bottom of your bag for an emergency. A poncho will fit over a backpack, keeping both you and your things dry.

- **Binoculars.** Use them to enhance the visual impact of any view. Look for a pair that is small, compact, and powerful.

- **Disposable cameras.** They're a good alternative to an expensive or heavy camera. I have been astonished at the high-quality photos they produce — particularly the panoramic version. My nephew gets great results from an underwater disposable. An expensive camera around the neck is the classic "I'm a tourist" signal; now you can avoid this trap.

- **Language translator.** With this amazing handheld gadget, you can have up to 14 languages at your fingertips, plus it converts metric and currency and stores personal names and numbers.

- **Kwikpoint™ folding cards.** These prove a picture is worth 1,000 words! Simply point to the picture of 600 colorful, universally recognized drawings to get your message across in any country (www.kwikpoint.com).

- **Swiss army knife or equivalent.** There are some really amazing tools available wherever knives or tools are sold. Decide exactly what tasks you want the knife to perform, then shop for those features. Prices vary with quality and number of features. Pack in checked baggage only.

- **Tool Logic™ Card.** This credit-card-sized holder contains some powerful little tools, similar to the knives above but so much smaller. (www.toollogic.com)

as thin as a credit card

- **Travel alarm clock.** Be sure it's dependable and small; both analog and digital models are available everywhere. Atomic clocks are the newest; they pick up radio signals from atomic time transmitters and reset themselves to maintain amazing accuracy across time zones.

- **Battery-operated book light.** If you love to read while your traveling companion sleeps, you'll be glad you packed one of these compact lights.

- **Flashlight.** Use one to navigate a strange and dark hotel room so you don't break a toe. (Broken toes from stumbling in the dark are the number one travel-related injury!) It's also a necessity if the power fails.

  - Look for the "no-battery" flashlights that can be cranked or shaken to recharge.

  - For camping or walking, the "Oval Light" illuminates both the path ahead and the ground at your feet with two separate beams (www.ovallight.com).

  - LED technology has created handy flashlights that use little energy and can't burn out. Available in traditional stick or mini-stick, key chain fob, or flat credit card shapes and sold in stores everywhere, there is no excuse for being in the dark!

- **Head lamp.** Lisa loves her hands-free light that straps to her head. She swears by it for camping, both for reading in bed and for following the path to the "outhouse." Look for this item in outdoor and camping stores.

- **Night light.** Plug into an entry or bathroom outlet to safely navigate a strange room. International versions are available at travel and luggage stores.

- **Rubber door wedge for low-tech but effective in-room security.** Or, look for a door stop alarm that wedges under the door and emits a shrill tone if disturbed.

SMART TRAVEL

Remove batteries and pack separately. That way, if the switch is bumped and accidentally turns on in transit, the batteries can't wear down. Pack extra batteries for all travel accessories as they can be difficult to purchase when traveling internationally. As of 1/1/08, lithium batteries must be installed in the electronic device inside checked luggage, not carried loose. Spare or loose batteries may be carried onboard if stored in the original packaging or in a plastic baggie.

SMART TRAVEL

It is a good idea to put your name on all of your travel accessories. I use little return address sticky labels to identify my camera, binoculars, sunglasses case, umbrella — everything. If I accidentally leave something behind, I know it had my name on it and it's more likely to find its way back to me.

Pack Things That Make You Happy!

Everyone has something from home that will make them happier and more comfortable on the go. Consider these ideas from fellow travelers.

- Marcy packs a scented candle to freshen stuffy hotel room air. Barbara W. takes an air freshener that plugs into an electrical outlet so she doesn't have to remember to blow out a candle — an especially good idea if you are prone to falling asleep in front of the TV.

- Sid takes names and addresses of friends on pre-addressed sticky labels so she can quickly send post cards. She leaves her bulky address book at home.

- June H. packs her own down pillow on her trips. She puts it in as the top layer in her Pullman-style suitcase and says it squashes down flat.

- Bill H. won't go anywhere without his pocket knife and you shouldn't either; a Swiss army knife (page 197) is even better. It comes in handy for lots of things, including being able to prepare exotic picnic meals from the unusual treats you can find in local grocery stores and markets. Pack in your checked baggage only.

- I travel with my picnic supplies: can opener, bottle opener, and corkscrew; plastic utensils, plastic or paper plates and bowls and paper napkins; plastic tablecloth (or yesterday's newspaper); blanket or emergency blanket (available at any sporting goods department) for picnics on the ground; soft insulated bag, collapsible cooler (or an inexpensive cooler purchased at my destination and left there upon departure).

CHAPTER 23

Stay Healthy and Happy

You can't have fun if you don't feel well —
take good care of yourself on the road.

If you are healthy and fit when you leave on your trip, the chances are better that you'll stay that way throughout your travels. The most common illnesses travelers experience are colds and diarrhea caused by exposure to unfamiliar bacteria and viruses. If you're healthy when you leave home, it's easier to fight off these potential problems.

Planning and organizing in advance for a healthful trip can help eliminate "last-minute stress syndrome." Just like Mom said: Get adequate rest, follow a good exercise program, eat a balanced diet, and take your vitamins.

Bring Your Medical Records

Before departure, prepare a medical history for yourself and for all family members traveling with you. Keep one copy with your valuable documents, one in your suitcase, and leave one at home with family or friends. It should include the following (add email addresses if traveling with a laptop):

1. Your name, address, and phone and fax numbers

2. Passport number(s)

3. Driver's license number(s)

4. All doctors' names, addresses, office and emergency phone and fax numbers

5. Health insurance provider, 24-hour phone and fax numbers, your policy and group or ID numbers

6. Your blood type(s)

7. Chronic health issues such as heart problems, high blood pressure, or diabetes

8. Any known allergies to medications, food, or environmental agents

9. Eyeglasses prescriptions

10. Name, address, and phone number of a family member or close friend to contact in case of an emergency

SMART TRAVEL Tip

Sid recommends exchanging copies of your medical information with your traveling companion in case of an emergency. Then pray it is never needed!

Pack a Take-Along Medicine Cabinet

When traveling, particularly internationally, it is very important to pack your own medications. There is nothing worse than being sick in a strange place without the medication that can help you feel better. It is difficult to buy an antihistamine in China when you don't speak Chinese and in some countries the product quality may be suspect.

Here is what I carry:

- Antacid
- Antibiotic cream
- Antihistamine
- Antiseptic
- Aspirin, acetaminophen, or ibuprofen
- Band-Aids, gauze pads, tape
- Cold medication
- Constipation remedy
- Diarrhea treatment (Imodium® A-D, Pepto-Bismol®, or Lomotil)
- Hydrocortisone cream
- Insect repellent
- Moleskin or 2nd Skin® Sport Blister Pads, or Band-Aid Blister Block Cushions.
- Motion sickness pills, wristbands (Sea Bands) or patch
- Nasal decongestant

- Prescriptions and vitamins; these can be counted out and packed in a small container for domestic travel. For international travel, it is wise to take medications in their original container and pack a copy of each prescription to prove you're not carrying illegal drugs, should authorities ask.
- Scissors (pack in checked baggage only)
- Spare eyeglasses; eyeglass repair kit
- Sunscreen
- Thermometer (mercury thermometers may be banned on international flights)
- Tweezers

SMART TRAVEL

Leslie packs her pills into a film canister; Joanne R. uses a compartmentalized box with one space per day. She recommends always taking two extra day's worth of any pills you need, just in case. For international travel, it is best to keep prescription drugs in their original containers as drug laws can be very strict.

Stay Healthy On the Road

To stay as healthy as possible, maintain as much of your at-home fitness program as possible while you travel. If you normally jog, pack your running clothes and ask at your motel/hotel desk for a map of a safe running route. If you swim, book a place with a pool and plan this into your schedule.

Portable exercise equipment includes jump ropes, plastic "weights" that you fill with water, and stretch bands. Some of my trips are so walking intensive, I don't need much more exercise!

Stay Healthy In-Flight

Sitting in cramped quarters for long stretches is bound to make any traveler cranky and uncomfortable. Try the following for a stress-free flight:

1. **Travel in loose and comfortable clothing** (see page 181).

2. **Move around as much as possible** to improve circulation and minimize the possibility of blood clots in the legs. Vascular specialists suggest taking aspirin before a long flight; it thins the blood and helps prevent clots. Request an aisle seat; it's easier to get up and take a walk every hour or so during flight (or more often if you don't have to disturb seatmates).

3. **Take off your shoes** (make sure to wear a pair that is loose enough so you can put them on again after your feet have swollen!) and elevate your feet by propping them up on a pillow or blanket, suitcase, briefcase or purse (see page 182). Do not cross your legs — it cuts off circulation.

4. **Avoid dehydration.** Sahara-like dry air with only 1-10% humidity can result in general discomfort, digestive problems, headaches, sinus problems, fatigue, and increased symptoms

of jet lag. Drink 8 ounces of water or other plain beverage for each hour of flight. Avoid alcoholic beverages, anything with caffeine, including soft drinks, or salty drinks like tomato juice; they only increase dehydration. I often carry my own bottled water so I have enough and don't have to pester the over-worked airline crew. Drinking so much liquid also forces you to walk frequently — to the bathroom.

Dry air also causes red, sore eyes. Adding artificial tear drops to your eyes several times during a flight brings great relief. Most frequent travelers wear glasses rather than contact lenses for comfort during long flights. If you must wear contacts in transit, soft or gas-permeable lenses breathe the best.

Super-dry air dries out upper respiratory passages, increasing susceptibility to infection. Keep nasal pas-sages moist by using a saline nasal spray every 2-3 hours.

To hydrate the skin, apply hand lotion frequently; use a good moisturizer before boarding and reapply during the flight. Use a spritzer bottle (Evian® atomizer) to refresh your face and hair. After arriving at your destination, take a steamy shower or bath to rehydrate your body and your upper respira-tory tract.

5. **Always fly with an inhaler handy if you are asthmatic.**

6. **Prevent ear pain during take off and landing by swallowing or chewing gum.** A decongestant taken before flight and again an hour before descent also helps, as does nasal spray 30 minutes before and during descent. EarPlanes™ (www.cirrushealthcare.com) are a product designed to relieve pain caused by rapid changes in cabin pressure. If none of these succeed, use the "flight-crew maneuver." Close your mouth, pinch your nose tightly, and try to blow through your pinched nose. This should cause your ears to pop. Repeat during descent.

7. **Use a personal air purifier** to cleanse cabin air in flight. Air Supply™ by Wein Products (www.magellans.com) substan-tially reduces pollutants, dust, smoke, pollen, germs and odors so fresh air is released toward your mouth, nose and eyes. Advocates claim fewer colds from re-circulated cabin air.

TEN TIPS FOR A HEALTHY BACK

If you are part of the 80% of the population with a significant back problem, and even if you're not, these tips are for you.

1. **Pack your suitcase on a higher surface than the bed** — the dining room table, a dresser, a kitchen counter. Reaching and twisting to pack on a low surface can cause back strain.

2. **Pack into two smaller bags;** they're easier to manage than one large one.

3. **Purchase luggage with wheels or use wheelies.**

4. **Tip a sky cap to lift your luggage.**

5. **Check your luggage.** Lifting a heavy bag into the overhead bin can aggravate back problems; so can trying to get it under the seat in front of you. Check luggage on trains and buses too.

6. **Use a small pillow to support your lower back and a neck pillow for your head.** When seated, your knees should be above your hips to take pressure off your back. Sit with your feet on a pillow or blanket or on top of your briefcase or purse. (See illustration on page 182).

7. **Slide your bags onto the back seat of your car** rather than lifting them up into or out of the trunk. If you must use the trunk, lift your bags carefully, then back away from the car and turn. *Don't lift and twist at the same time!*

8. **Adjust the car seat so that your knees are slightly bent.** A lumbar pillow or built-in lumbar adjustment in the seat also helps.

9. **Stop every hour or so to take a walking break** if you are driving. If traveling by plane, get up to stretch your legs several times during the flight.

10. **Request a firm mattress** when you make your hotel reservation.

Minimize Jet Lag

Jet lag is a major complaint, particularly on international trips. Although you can't eliminate it entirely, there are several things you can do to minimize it.

1. **Start your trip well rested.** Begin a gradual transition to your new time zone before you leave. For example, go to bed an hour earlier and rise an hour earlier if you are heading east. This is more helpful when traveling from coast to coast than from continent to continent.

2. **Switch to your destination time zone when you get on the plane.** Sleep and eat accordingly to get into the rhythm of the new time zone more quickly.

3. **Avoid alcohol and drink plenty of water. Eat lightly,** avoiding salty, rich, and fatty foods. If meals are served, request a special meal from the airline at least 24 hours in advance; the low fat or seafood meals are nice. Do exercises in your seat or get up and move around as much as possible

4. **Make yourself comfortable** so you can get some sleep on the plane. Use all possible aids to achieve this — see page 183 for suggestions.

5. **Many find that "No-Jet-Lag" helps.** This homeopathic tablet helps to ease jet lag symptoms, has no side effects and is compatible with other medications. My husband and I have used it many times — we feel better when we take No-Jet-Lag than when we do not. (www.nojetlag.com)

6. **Schedule your travel so you can take a flight that arrives at night,** if at all possible. Stay awake for as long as you can during the flight, nap on board, then go to bed at a reasonable hour after checking into your hotel and unpacking.

7. **Reset your body clock** if you have arrived during the morning by not going to sleep immediately. Go out for a daylight stroll for an hour or two, have a snack, and then return to your room after noon to nap for a short time. When you wake up, it will be time for dinner and a normal evening, followed by bedtime at 11:00 or so.

8. **Plan a light work or tourist schedule for the first full day** to give your body time to rest and recover from a long trip. Doctors recommend one day or more of rest for each time zone crossed, which is a great idea in concept but often difficult in reality.

Plan For A Healthful International Trip

When traveling internationally, think about health issues well in advance. Have all regular medical check-ups prior to travel. What is routine care at home can become a costly medical emergency in a foreign country. Get dental work done before departure. Small cavities can erupt into excruciating toothaches during high-altitude flights.

Ask your doctor to refer you to a travel specialist or clinic for the latest information on required inoculations and health issues in the area where you plan to travel. There are now more than 500 travel clinics in the US. Their specialized training is in tropical medicine, international health and infectious diseases, and wilderness medicine. They recommend an appointment 4 to 6 weeks prior to departure because some immunities take time to develop.

The major hospitals in my city have travel clinics that provide:

• Immunizations for diseases such as yellow fever and hepatitis

• Medications/prescriptions for preventing malaria (the leading cause of illness and death in the developing world), motion sickness, diarrhea, and other possible problems

• Post-travel follow-up for conditions such as rashes, fever, and jet lag

Travelers who don't have the proper vaccines required for entry into developing countries may be quarantined and forced to get shots at the border, possibly administered by a border guard who doesn't have disposable syringes.

A directory of physicians in the US and Canada who specialize in travelers' health and tropical medicine is available free from the American Society of Tropical Medicine and Hygiene (see "Resources," page 239). You can also do research on your own by checking with the Centers for Disease Control and Prevention (CDC). They operate a free travelers' hotline that includes information on vaccinations. Websites for CDC, the World Health Organization, and the International Society of Travel Medicine are listed in "Resources," beginning on page 237.

Heads-Up Health Tips

Water

A *Conde Nast Traveler* survey revealed only one-third of the world's nations have tap water considered safe to drink. For travelers, that means drinking the local water is likely to make you sick. Generally, the more tropical and populous and the poorer a region is, the higher the risk of contracting something even more serious than "travelers' diarrhea."

1. **Avoid problems by drinking only bottled water.** The CDC recommends carbonated water over flat water because it is harder to tamper with and its slightly acidic nature helps inhibit bacterial growth. Choose brand names you know whenever possible and make sure that all bottled water arrives sealed and is opened in your presence.

   In *A Journey of One's Own*, author Thalia Zepatos recounts a telling story: "After drinking the 'filtered water' for a week at a guesthouse on the beach in Oaxaca, I got up early one morning to witness the filtration process. A young woman held a dirty dishrag over the end of the garden hose to fill the container. It did catch the pebbles and insects..."

SMART TRAVEL *Gadget*

If you are traveling to a region with questionable water and doubt your ability to buy safe bottled water, purchase a personal water purification system before you leave home. These health-saving products will purify water from any source, from faucets to mountain streams. The Katadyn® Extstream is a practical drinking bottle with an integrated water filter (www.katadyn.us), Micropur® from Katadyn is a convenient non-iodine water purification tablet, or the SteriPEN™ purifies water using Ultraviolet (UV) light (www.steripen.com). Look for these products in travel catalogs and online and in camping/outdoor stores.

2. **Avoid ice cubes.** If the water isn't safe, ice will not be safe either. Use ice to chill a container; don't put the ice into the liquid. Wipe off cans and bottles carefully; even a few drops of unclean water can cause illness. Use a straw when drinking from a can or bottle.

SMART TRAVEL *Gadget*

Jerry J. suggests packing your own collapsible cup to share drinks but not germs.

3. **Use bottled water when brushing your teeth and rinsing your toothbrush.** Do not swallow any water while showering or swimming.

4. **Hot drinks made with boiling water are safe to drink.** Avoid using milk or cream in tea or coffee unless it is in sealed individual containers that have been kept cold.

Food

I am very cautious about what I eat when traveling, even though I love food. I survived food poisoning once and never want to repeat the experience. As with water purity, the risk of food being unclean and making you sick is generally higher in tropical, crowded, and poor areas.

Choose busy restaurants (all of those patrons can't be wrong) that look clean and opt for made-to-order dishes rather than buffet items that may have been sitting for long periods at an unsafe temperature.

In many countries, street food is so tempting — it smells wonderful and is usually very cheap. Eat at your own risk. Sheila must

SAFE FOODS (at least most likely to be so) include:

- fruits that are easily peeled or that can be sliced open without contamination
- freshly baked breads

- fresh, **fully cooked** hot dishes, served hot
- packaged or canned foods

UNSAFE FOODS (at least most likely to be so) include:

- shellfish and seafood
- raw or under-cooked beef, pork, sausage, or fish (ceviche)
- cold foods, salads, and raw vegetables (may contain impure water and have greater risk of contamination from the hands of infected food handlers)
- buffet dishes and foods left out at room temperatures
- sauces left out on the table

- milk and milk products unless you are positive they were pasteurized and have been handled properly
- custards, cream pastries, cream sauces, and anything made with mayonnaise
- foods stored and reheated after cooking (lasagna) or cooked and served at room temperature (quiche)
- unpeelable fruits or fruits peeled by others

have a cast-iron stomach — she successfully ate street food throughout Southeast Asia and loved it. I am very selective; I avoid anything that is not quick-cooked before my eyes. In Asia I choose stir-fried noodles with vegetables because high heat kills bacteria. I eat no meat — the food vendors have been in the heat for hours with no way to keep raw foods cold. Single-use, disposable paper or plastic plates are safest; I watched a street vendor rinse her dishes in cold tap water on the sidewalk and she called them clean! I always take my own paper-wrapped, disposable chopsticks or plastic utensils. Utensils that you carefully wash yourself are also OK.

My bout with food poisoning is nothing compared to other diseases you can get from food. Hepatitis A is a viral infection of the liver spread by fecal contamination of food and water and is constantly present in many of the world's most appealing travel destinations. It is spread through unclean food-handling practices and the risks are highest in poor, tropical countries where the standard of hygiene is low and the water is unsafe. Expensive hotels offer some protection if they are diligent about safe food handling and hygiene practices but remember that the staff all goes home — to possibly poor local hygiene.

PAY ATTENTION TO THIS!

Hepatitis A is now completely preventable with new vaccines that provide 100% protection for at least ten years. Two doses are required, one 4 to 6 weeks prior to travel and the other within six months to one year (depending on the drug used). **No traveler can afford to ignore this vital hepatitis A vaccine.** Ask your doctor and insist on being protected.

You don't have to be traveling internationally to be exposed to Hepatitis A. JoAnne and Dave were 75 miles away from home and stopped in a fast food restaurant for a snack. Both contracted Hepatitis A; they were very ill for a month and recovery took weeks after that. In adults there is a two percent risk of liver failure and a death rate of one in 250, so treat this illness with respect.

Travelers' Diarrhea

According to The American Society of Tropical Medicine and Hygiene, travelers' diarrhea affects approximately 30-40% of travelers to the developing world, with contaminated food, water and beverages being the most common sources of infection. Following the above suggestions for water and food will help improve your chances of avoiding this common problem, as will careful and frequent hand washing.

Should you become a victim, the first line of treatment is to replace lost fluids and electrolytes. Drink plenty of pure water, decaffeinated tea or carbonated beverages, broth, or juice. If diarrhea has been a problem during past travels or you typically have a sensitive tummy consider packing oral rehydration salts such as Ceralyte® (www.ceraproducts.com), or, for children, Pedialyte® (www.pedialyte.com). Consult with your doctor or local travel clinic for advice and diarrhea fighting prescriptions before you leave home.

Insects

Bites or stings from mosquitoes, fleas, ticks, and flies are more than just itchy; they can cause painful irritation or debilitating and sometimes deadly diseases. Malaria, Lyme's disease, dengue, yellow fever, Rocky Mountain spotted fever, plague, and West Nile Virus are all extremely serious insect-borne diseases. The CDC can tell you if you are venturing into a problem area so you can prepare yourself. Even though no current anti-malarial drug guarantees protection against malaria, you can help yourself avoid it by doing your best to prevent mosquito bites.

Apply insect repellent to your hands first and then rub onto your skin. Use it liberally and frequently, covering all exposed areas (avoiding the eyes and mouth) — insects can detect an unprotected area the size of a dime! Wear light-colored, long-sleeved shirts, tuck long pants into your socks, and avoid perfume and scented toiletries when venturing into areas with concentrated insect populations. Spray your outer clothing with repellent as well. BUZZ OFF clothing is a new alternative to spraying your clothing with repellent. (See page 152 for more information.) Insect repellent for your room and a mosquito net for sleeping are important in some areas.

Natural insect repellents work for some (but need to be reapplied every 1-2 hours). Test several formulations to see if they work for you. Daily doses of vitamin B-1 are a natural mosquito repellent for others. Picaridin is the best-selling European and Australian ingredient, newly available in the US. It is highly effective, safe even for young children and people with DEET sensitivity.

Since insects view me as filet mignon, I choose a repellent with 20 to 35 % DEET (DEET and Picaridin are the most effective ingredients according to the CDC). Higher concentrations of DEET, even though they will last longer, can cause skin irritation for some. DEET concentration of 35% lasts 4 to 6 hours, 100% DEET lasts up to 10 hours. Reapply as needed.

I carry a small lipstick-style insect repellent in my purse when I am in buggy areas. Repellent towelettes are also handy. Be diligent about using insect repellent no matter where you are going. I got the itchiest mosquito bite I can remember while inside a store in Shanghai. Pack an itch relief product such as calamine lotion or hydrocortisone cream too.

Camping and sporting goods stores or departments are good sources for serious insect repellents.

CHAPTER 24

Be Savvy and Safe

Being a responsible traveler is your job, so take charge.

Savvy travelers plan ahead to minimize problems and maximize fun. The greatest danger to travelers is petty theft, says *Conde Nast Traveler*. The most frequent site of a crime according to people in their poll who had been robbed:

44%: items taken from a hotel room
26%: street snatchings
17%: from a car
16%: at an airport
3%: each in airplanes and cruise cabins
(Adds up to greater than 100% as some respondents reported more than one incident.)

With this advance information, how can you best plan to hold on to your possessions while traveling? First review "Worldwide Wardrobing" beginning on page 36 for guidance on planning your travel wardrobe so you blend in rather than stand out as a tourist and a target. This is your first line of defense.

Before You Leave Home

My purse was stolen from under the seat of the locked car on the first day of my first trip to Europe. I lost my passport, driver's license, travelers checks — everything. It cost me two full days of travel to go to the nearest embassy (a city not on my itinerary) plus the time and money spent acquiring the replacement passport. I had taken none of the precautions below and paid the price. I travel smarter and safer today!

1. **Make copies of the inside cover and first page of your passport.** The inside cover contains your photo, date of birth, date of issue and expiration, passport number, and other coded information. A copy will help establish your identity at an embassy or consulate. Hide copies in different pieces of luggage. It's a good idea to carry an extra set of passport photos as well.

2. **Make copies of electronic airline tickets and confirmation numbers and hide them, too.** With the ticket numbers, airlines can more easily reissue lost or stolen tickets. Without them, you will have to purchase a new ticket, possibly at full fare, and wait for a refund.

3. **Make photocopies of your driver's license, credit and debit cards, the serial numbers on traveler's checks, phone cards, and other documents you're taking along.** Also write down toll-free phone numbers for canceling stolen or lost credit cards and to replace traveler's checks. Make sure you have international toll-free numbers if you are going out of the country.

4. **Leave copies of all of the above information, along with a copy of your itinerary, at home** with a family member, at your office, or with a trusted friend — someone who can be reached easily if you need them.

5. **Check expiration dates on your passport, credit cards, and driver's license.** Remove unnecessary credit cards from your wallet. Your Sears charge card will *not* be of any help to you in Hong Kong.

At Your Hotel

We'd all like to think that a locked suitcase inside a locked hotel room is a safe place to hide valuables, but in fact it's not. To feel safe in your home away from home:

1. **Don't take it with you if you don't really need it!** Then you won't have to worry about keeping valuables secure.

2. **Check out the safety of your hotel neighborhood before you go** — ask your travel agent, a city resident, or a friend who's been there before.

3. **Choose a hotel or motel with interior hallways and one or two monitored entrances;** they're the most secure. Hotels and motels with unmonitored exterior hallway doors are easy targets. Those with rooms opening onto an exterior walkway are the least secure.

4. **Ask for a room on floors 3 to 6.** These floors are high enough to prevent easy access from the ground and low enough to be reached by fire equipment.

5. **Ask the hotel clerk to write down your room number** instead of announcing it when you register. If it is shouted out, ask for another room. Keep room keys out of view in the restaurant, on the elevator, and at the pool to prevent key theft or wandering eyes from reading the numbers. If your room key disappears, ask for a new room or for the electronic lock to be re-keyed. Card keys for electronic door locks cannot be duplicated; the codes are changed for every guest. This type of keying system is the best protection.

6. **Use all available locks when you are in your room** — door lock, dead bolt, *and* safety chain. Make sure that any doors to connecting rooms are locked. I travel with a small rubber, wedge-shaped doorstop that makes it almost impossible to push a door open—easier than putting a chair under the knob!

SMART TRAVEL *Gadget*

Several different types of add-on portable door locks are worth investigating; look at your local hardware store or travel and luggage retail store, catalog, or online. They are handy for those charming bed and breakfasts and small inns that often don't have adequate door locks and will deter the overly aggressive maid or innkeeper.

7. **Make sure your sliding glass door locks and has a security bar.** If not, request another more secure room.

8. **Use the door peephole!** Ask hotel employees to show ID and view it through the peephole. Verify deliveries to your room with the front desk before letting someone in. Check with the hotel if a repair person asks to work while you are there.

9. **Have your key in your hand before entering the hotel elevator.** Fumbling for keys makes you vulnerable and you cannot give your full attention to other elevator occupants.

10. **Hang the "Do Not Disturb" sign on your door and leave the TV on when you leave. Do not use the "Maid Please Clean Room" sign** — everyone will know you're not in.

11. **Lock your suitcase (yours does lock, doesn't it?) whenever you leave the room.** It will not keep out the serious thief but will thwart the casually tempted. Remember to always take a bag lock with you, even though airline security now prohibits locking your bag.

12. **Use the room safe or the hotel safe** at the front desk to store your valuables — cash, jewelry, travel documents, camera, camcorder, and laptop. The smartest move of all? Leave your valuables at home if at all possible.

On the Street

Tourists are easy targets on busy streets in strange locales so it's essential to pay attention while you enjoy the sites. Here's how to be street smart and safe.

1. **Dress as inconspicuously as possible;** try to blend with the local population. Do not wear anything that announces your nationality. Tourists are thought to be wealthy and naive and are viewed as easy targets. *Remember, tourist = target.*

2. **Keep your essential valuables (passport, airline ticket, money, traveler's checks, credit and debit cards, and card receipts containing your card number) on your person at all times in a money belt or a security wallet worn under your clothing.** All of the following security wallets will protect your valuables — you decide which will be most comfortable for you to wear.

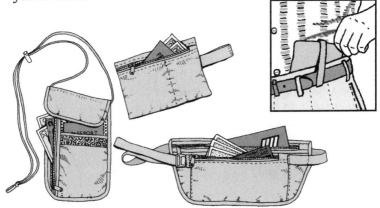

If you wear a waistbelt-style security wallet under your clothing, it may look less bulky and feel more comfortable placed at the small of your back.

3. **Use interior zippered pockets for valuables;** these are quite secure. Many travel catalogs feature good-looking clothing with zippered inside pockets (see page 42 for some examples). If you sew, you can add inside pockets to your clothes. You'll also want to check out the travel wear patterns offered by SAF-T-POCKETS™ (see "Resources" page 238).

SMART TRAVEL Tip

If you must carry a traditional wallet, place it in a front pants pocket or an inside coat pocket. Place a rubber band around your wallet to make it more difficult for a pickpocket to slide it out of a pocket unnoticed. Ditto with a passport.

4. **Keep only a small amount of cash for each day in your shoulder bag, or your front pants pocket, or a waist pack worn in the front.** A photographer's vest with multiple pockets is good in casual dress situations.

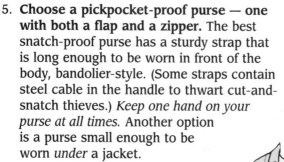

5. **Choose a pickpocket-proof purse — one with both a flap and a zipper.** The best snatch-proof purse has a sturdy strap that is long enough to be worn in front of the body, bandolier-style. (Some straps contain steel cable in the handle to thwart cut-and-snatch thieves.) *Keep one hand on your purse at all times.* Another option is a purse small enough to be worn *under* a jacket.

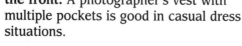

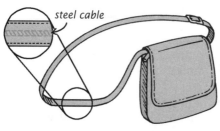

steel cable

6. **Wear your purse at all times. Do not take it off, no matter where you are** — in the bathroom, in the restaurant during lunch, in the theater. Roz and I watched a potential disaster unfold in a New York City coffee shop when a group of men entered and created a diversion. The man nearest the door reached for a woman's purse that was casually hanging over the back of her chair. The path was clear to the subway station just outside. This snatch was foiled by another patron who saw what was happening and shouted "Watch out! He's grabbing your purse!" The men dashed for the subway station empty-handed and the near-victim tourist was very grateful.

   Ann thought she was being helpful by giving directions to travelers in front of her hotel. Unfortunately, as she put her purse down on the ground to have both hands free to hold the map, another part of the diversion team snatched her bag and ran. If you must put your purse or backpack on the ground, put your foot through the strap.

7. **Get clear directions to your destination.** Ask for written directions as well as maps at your hotel and memorize your route. Reading a map on the street corner is a good clue that you're lost and a prime target. Barbara W. lost $200 in cash in Paris when a kindly soul (she thought) stopped to give her directions and she opened her bag to retrieve her map. If you need help, look for a police officer or pop into a business for assistance.

8. **Pick up a hotel business card and keep it with you at all times** so you know the name, address, and phone number. In a foreign country, ask for one in both English and the local language. There is nothing more frustrating or less secure than trying to describe to a taxi driver the hotel you want to go to when neither of you speak the same language. If the card has a map on it, that's even better; a picture is worth a thousand words!

9. **Keep your camera out of sight;** don't wear it dangling from your neck or wrist. Someone can grab it or cut the strap in a flash! Avoid expensive camera bags, too. An opaque plastic shopping bag from a local market in the town you're visiting makes the most inconspicuous camera bag. Consider using an inexpensive or disposable camera instead of the pricey one you use at home.

In Your Car

Just because you can lock the doors, don't assume your car is safe from devious thieves, even when you're in it!

1. **Do not do leave your purse "hidden" under the seat of the car,** as I did. Thieves know to look there first.

2. **Do not leave anything of value in your car.** If you must leave your possessions in your car, lock them in the trunk. However, a trunk is not safe if there is a trunk release latch inside the car! Do not stop at a roadside attraction, open the trunk, and lock your purse inside. It is very easy for a thief to pop open your trunk and remove the goodies he saw you place there.

3. **Ask for a rental car that has a secure trunk** rather than a hatchback where contents are visible.

4. **Make sure your rental car is free of rental company stickers and special license plates.** You want to look like a local. *Remember, tourist = target.*

5. **Remove all "I am tourist" indicators** — maps, travel guides, etc. — from view.

SMART TRAVEL

Place a local grocery bag or a local newspaper in full view inside your car to give it the appearance of a local vehicle.

6. **Back your car into a parking space** if that makes out-of-state license plates less obvious.

7. **Take all contents of your car inside to your hotel room.** If you are using a clothing rod that hangs across the back seat, *take all hanging items into your room.* John, a well-dressed traveling salesman, went out to his car to select an outfit for the day and found his entire wardrobe of expensive suits, sport coats, pants, and perfectly ironed shirts gone. Even though his car was parked three feet from the door of his room, the car was empty.

8. **Do not place valuables in plain sight** — on the dash or in the back window, for example, even when you're in the car. Becky and Sam were robbed while in their car by a bold bicycle thief who smashed the window and grabbed a handbag!

9. **Lock the car doors,** even when you're in the car. When traveling in your own vehicle, don't forget to use your car alarm or "The Club®'" to prevent car theft.

In the Travel Terminal

Travelers using major transportation centers around the world, international airports in particular, have found themselves victims of teams of professional thieves. The best defense is to be aware and stay 100% focused on your surroundings and your belongings. Pay attention: Did the doorman accidentally load your bag in the wrong car (as happened to Marilyn R. M.); did the cab driver leave one of your bags at the curb?

1. **Keep your eyes and preferably a hand on your carry-ons at all times.** Thieves know that savvy travelers stow their valuables in their carry-on luggage. Therefore, it becomes a prime target in plane, train, and bus terminals as well as restaurants. Expensive designer bags and laptop computers attract thieves' attention first, but don't think they won't take less promising carry-ons as well.

2. **Travel light.** The fewer pieces of carry-on you have, the less you have to keep track of.

3. **Mark your bags well.**

   • Place an ID tag on *every* bag, carry-ons included. The best tags have a cover over your name. This cover could be a photo of you — proof of ownership in any language. Use your business rather than home address for even more protection. Use your cell phone number so you can be located while traveling.

   • Place identification inside your bag in case the outside tag is lost.

   • Include a copy of your itinerary in an outside zippered pocket or inside your bag. It will help your lost or stolen bag find you, even without proper tagging.

- Mark your bag so you can recognize it faster. Distinctive marks also emphasize ownership (see pages 97-98).

- Take a color photo of your luggage with you or take a picture with your cell phone or digital camera so you can remember what it looks like. You can show it to baggage attendants to identify missing pieces. Write the brand name and bag sizes on the back.

4. **Keep your eyes on your bags on the shuttle buses and in the parking lot.** Be especially aware at stops — did the driver just off-load your bag at United instead of American? Be conscious of your carry-on too; it should remain in your lap while you sit or between your feet if you're standing and cannot hold it.

5. **Do not leave curbside check-in until you see your checked bags go safely onto the conveyor belt or into the airport** with a sky cap. If your bags are placed on an unsupervised cart, a well-dressed thief could easily remove them from the cart. Adequate tips to sky caps help ensure their attention to your bags.

6. **Place your carry-on bag between your feet and in front of you at the check-in counter.** Place a briefcase or purse on the counter in front of you and hold onto it!

7. **Keep your carry-on with you at all times.** In the bathroom, I select a stall next to a wall and wheel my bag with me, then place my bag next to the wall. I keep my shoulder bag around my neck and use the hook for only my coat.

(continued on page 222)

SMART TRAVEL *Gadget*

If you have a long layover and need to sleep in an airport, train, or bus station, use a cable lock to secure your belongings to your chair or your body.

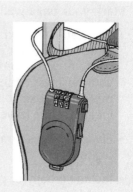

Use the following tips to pass through the security screening station in terminals.

PAY ATTENTION TO THIS!

Although terminal theft is lower because over-all security is increased, you are vulnerable at these checkpoints and vigilance is important. Teams of professional thieves are good at dropping coins or spilling coffee to create a diversion so they can steal items right off the conveyor belt — even right out of the scanning box!

- Out of view and before entering the screening area, remove jewelry, belts, coins, keys, etc. that you think might set off the metal detector. Place them securely inside your carry-on bag.

- Stand in line with your carry-on in front of you. Be alert.

- Place your belongings on the belt with any openings toward the front so that a thief cannot reach in and remove an item from your bag. If you have several items, put smaller items on first in a security bin, followed by the largest. Lynn wraps her purse strap through the handles of her other carry-on's so her items are "tied" together.

- Pause if possible before walking through the electronic gate to give your carry-on items time to enter the scanner box. Your belongings are a prime target for theft if you are delayed and they go through the scanner before you get through it.

- If you set off the metal detector and are asked to step aside for a hand-wand search, request permission to stand so you can keep an eye on your belongings or ask a traveling partner to monitor or retrieve your things

- Don't forget to retrieve your valuables! Every day hundreds of cell phones and laptops are left at security checkpoints.

(continued from page 220)

8. **Place your belongings in your lap, on the bench (if there is one) next to the wall, or securely between your feet when using a pay phone or your cell phone in a phone "booth".** If using your cell phone in a boarding area, keep your belongings between your feet and your eyes on your things!

9. **Label all of your belongings,** and I do mean all. From PDA to cell phone to camera to laptop, cables, adapters and cords, label it all with name, cell phone number, and email address. This way, you stand a chance for lost or stolen items to be returned.

10. **Keep information secure and private by using a privacy filter on your laptop screen.** The person seated next to you in the boarding area or on the plane who is sneaking a peek at your screen will see nothing from the side, but the image is clear to you when viewed straight on. Keep cell phone calls private by moving yourself (and your belongings) to a less populated area, and don't discuss anything you wouldn't want your mother to overhear.

11. **Listen to the excellent CD "Traveler Beware" by Detective Kevin Coffey** (see Resources page 240). You will gasp at the boldness of thieves and how naive many of us are. Kevin literally shocks his listeners into becoming more conscious travelers.

CHAPTER 25

Money Matters

You can't spend what you don't have —
make sure you have the right kinds of money.

When you're traveling, having the "right money" matters. You need to plan for cash and credit on the road as well as for emergencies. I will never forget having to call a friend's husband to bail us out of a restaurant in New York City that did not take credit cards or checks. While "cash only" is a rarity in most places, it can happen. It's relatively easy to plan for domestic travel; international travel is another thing. Be sure to read "Be Savvy and Safe" beginning on page 212 to learn how to keep your money safe, both domestically and internationally.

For Domestic Travel

For domestic travel, go prepared for anything. I take cash, two credit cards, and an ATM card on domestic trips. My checkbook goes too or, at the least, I tuck a couple of checks in my wallet. I don't ever want a replay of the restaurant bail out!

For International Travel

Making financial transactions in other parts of the world may be different than here at home. At the least, you need to know how to deal with exchange rates, local currency, and foreign ATM machines.

What to Take with You

1. **Take a mix of cash, credit and debit cards, and only a few traveler's checks** as not many merchants still readily accept them. Transaction fees are high, counterfeits are common, and you may have to go to a bank to cash them. However, ATM machines do not work during a power outage but traveler's checks can be cashed. If you have access to free traveler's checks, have them issued in US dollars but be aware that you may be charged a fee when you use one for payment.

2. **Take some US $1 bills in addition to a small amount of cash** for airport expenses at each end of the trip. In a pinch, you can tip anywhere in the world with dollar bills.

3. **Take no more than two credit cards and an ATM card**. Locate ATM machines at your destination by checking on-line before leaving the US. Also take a couple of personal checks with you. If necessary, you can cash a check at a bank or an American Express office.

4. **Look for the newest option: a prepaid plastic "money card" available from credit card companies**. Buy a card loaded with a specific amount of money before you leave home and choose a PIN (personal identification number). Use the card to withdraw cash in local currency at an ATM machine.

Getting Local Currency

One of the first things you'll need when you reach your final destination is local currency. Here's how, when, and where to get it.

1. **Wait until you reach your destination** — unless you are arriving in the middle of the night. Most guidebooks suggest changing some money before departure from the US so you have cab fare and tip money to get you to your first hotel. Foreign exchange in the US is expensive. If you must exchange at home, change only enough for the afore-mentioned expenses.

2. **Change some money at the foreign exchange at the border, airport, or train station.** Generally, when the airport or station is open, this booth is open. Again, change only a small amount to get you to your hotel, for tips, and for immediate expenses. Then take the time to compare rates at local banks to acquire larger sums of local currency for a few days or the length of your stay in that country.

Getting the Best Exchange Rate

Listed from generally the best rate to worst rate:

BEST RATE 1. **Using your credit card to charge is the way to get the very best exchange rate.** With a credit card, the transaction will be converted at the "wholesale" exchange rate that banks use for large-scale transactions. Credit card companies and banks are now each adding on fees for foreign transactions. Check with your providers to determine which of your cards charge the lowest, if any, fees.

2. The next best rate of exchange is to use an ATM machine. If your ATM card works in the Cirrus or Plus network at home, you will be able to withdraw cash from foreign bank ATM's that are part of these networks. You receive local currency and the machine debits your bank account at home using the wholesale rate.

You can exchange cash or traveler's checks for local currency at the following places:

3. Cashing a traveler's check at a branch of the company that issued it, i.e., cashing an American Express check at the local AMEX office

4. Bank currency exchange window (change cash or cash a traveler's check)

5. Bank currency exchange window that assesses a fee per check or a percentage of the transaction

6. Hotel cashier desks — an expensive service for guests

7. Privately run exchange businesses; these are often open when banks are closed. You will usually pay dearly for this convenience.

8. Paying for a purchase with foreign currency or traveler's checks in a shop or restaurant and asking them to become the exchange. I quote a waiter in Strasbourg: "But Monsieur, zis is not ze bank!"

WORST RATE 9. Cash advances on credit cards; these incur interest charged from the date of the advance until you pay the bill, plus a transaction fee or a percentage of the advance. This can be **very** expensive.

It pays to compare the exchange rates and factor in any fees to see who is offering the best deal. The difference can be from five to ten percent. That amount gets my attention.

USING FOREIGN ATMs

Foreign ATMs do not all work the same as they do at home. Read these tips to make sure your card will work when you need cash.

- Many ATMs outside the US have numbers only. If your PIN number contains letters, convert using standard letters to numbers as they are positioned on US telephones. Do this at home so you don't panic at the machine.

- Many ATMs do not accept PINs with more than four digits. Ask your bank in advance for a four-digit PIN.

- Many ATMs automatically deduct funds from your primary account; they do not allow you to choose an account at the machine. Before traveling, go into your bank and ask which of your accounts is your primary one and make sure you have enough money in that account for your trip.

- Be prepared. Finding a participating ATM may not always be easy and your card may not work at all locations. Have other sources of funds available. Check with the bank that issued your ATM card for exact international locations before deciding to depend on new technology. As a rule, ATMs and credit cards are best for major cities; traveler's checks and cash are best for smaller areas.

- Locate ATM machines before you travel by checking these websites:
  http://visa.via.infonow.net/locator/global/jsp/SearchPage.jsp
  http://www.mastercard.com/us/personal/en/cardholder
     services/atmlocations/index.html

Take Heed

Here are a few other financial considerations to think about before you leave for an international trip.

1. **Call your credit card company before making an international trip** to determine their current policy about international currency exchange surcharges. Banks have charged 2% to 3% in fees, cancelled the charges, and then instituted them again. It is difficult to keep track!

2. **Make sure that you have high enough credit limits on your cards** to cover what you expect to spend.

3. **Minimize the number of exchange and ATM transactions you will need to make** by taking out larger sums each time you use the machine. This is particularly important if you are paying a flat fee for each transaction at an exchange or bank, or if your ATM card has a per-use fee for using an ATM elsewhere in the network.

4. **Take along a pocket calculator or a currency converter (see page 196) to calculate the local exchange rate.** It also comes in handy for "serious shopping." I learned a great trick from my world traveler husband: En route to a new country he takes out a business card and on the back creates an "at-a-glance" approximate exchange table. If I am browsing and curious about a price, I can glance at my card without dragging out the calculator.

With the card, I quickly learn financial relationships so when I shop I am not thinking something is equal to $10 when it is really closer to $100! When I am serious about making a purchase, I use my currency converter to make an exact calculation.

You can now print a convenient conversion chart in the currency of your choice from www.oanda.com/convert/cheatsheet.

Hong Kong Dollars	
HK $	US $
1	.13
10	1.30
50	6.50
100	13.00
200	26.00
300	39.00
400	52.00
500	65.00
1000	130.00
1500	195.00
2000	260.00
5000	650.00
7500	975.00
10,000	1,300.00

4. **Make sure the international retailer charges you in the local currency and does NOT charge you in the currency of your home country.** "Dynamic currency conversion", as this is called, is sold as a convenience, when it actually provides the merchant with the opportunity to use an inflated exchange rate and to pocket the difference at your expense.

The Euro €

It is now possible to travel to 15 countries in Europe and use the same currency — the Euro € — in all. More countries will be added to the "Eurozone" in the future. The euro is divided into 100 cents. There are seven euro notes that change in both size and color — as the value gets larger so does the size, and eight coins that get both larger and thicker as the value increases. Notes come in 5, 10, 20, 50, 200, and 500 values; coins range from 1 cent to 2 euros.

This is a blessing for travelers who will no longer need to change currency at every border. It is also believed that this will create greater price competition between the countries involved.

Three major members of the European Union still use their own currency: Great Britain (British Pound), Denmark (Danish Krone) and Sweden (Swedish Krona).

Returning Home

Before returning to the US, convert your foreign coins and bills into US dollars. If you wait to do this at home, the fees from your local bank or exchange will eat at least half of your money. I convert funds at my departing airport after paying any required airport departure taxes and checking the status of my flight. If the flight is running late, I may need local currency for lunch or a snack or for shopping. David once bailed out a sobbing American businesswoman at Tokyo's Narita airport. She ran out of cash and was about to miss her flight home because she had no Japanese yen for her departure tax. He paid her tax and she made her flight and immediately mailed him the money.

When changing money anywhere, local coins are often left over as most exchanges deal in paper foreign money only and not in bulky coins. I either bring my coins home to a coin-collecting kid or drop them in a conveniently placed charity box at my point of departure.

CHAPTER 26

Travel Insurance

*Depending on your circumstances, paying for
contingencies may make sense. Check your options.*

For your own peace of mind, consider the types of insurance
coverage you may need. Your medical policy may or may not
cover you while traveling and you may want trip insurance to
guard against financial loss should a tour or cruise be canceled.
Talk about insurance with your travel agent, but be aware that
insurance is a profit center for their beleaguered industry. For
information about insuring your possessions while traveling, see
below and "Checking or Carrying Bags?," page 93.

Medical Insurance

1. **Review your current health policies** to determine if your
   policy or HMO covers you while you are traveling. Note the
   exclusions:

   • Make sure you will be covered wherever you travel; some
   policies have geographic restrictions. Medicare doesn't
   cover any foreign charges; some supplements do, but you
   may need an additional travel policy.

   • Some exclude coverage if you are traveling to a country that
   the United States government has listed in a travel advisory.

   • Some exclude extreme sports such as mountain climbing.

   • Pregnant women close to delivery are often excluded from
   coverage while traveling.

2. **Be sure your travel documents include your health insurance provider information and an insurance claim form** for
   the attending physician should you need medical care while
   you're away from home.

3. **Join IAMAT — the International Association for Medical
   Assistance to Travelers** (see "Resources," page 239) if you are
   traveling to an area where English is not widely spoken and
   there is a chance you might need medical care. This is a
   non-profit organization; membership is free but a donation is

welcome. IAMAT compiles a worldwide directory of English and French-speaking doctors. They must meet IAMAT standards, agree to charge a specific fee, and be on 24-hour call.

Trip Insurance

If you are taking a tour or cruise and illness or an accident occurs before or during your trip, you could lose your advance payments or face very expensive emergency transportation costs. Luckily, trip insurance can protect you. However, insurance is the most overpriced of all travel services. Unless there's a good chance you'll have to cancel at the last minute — and possibly forfeit your entire prepayment — it may not be the best investment.

Experts suggest buying travel insurance only to cover risks you can't afford to absorb. Buy policies from an insurance company instead, not from the tour or cruise operator. If the tour/cruise operator fails, the insurance won't pay off.

Look at insurance purchased on a per trip basis. Investigate trip-cancellation, trip-interruption, trip-delay, medical, and baggage insurance. The types you choose and how much coverage you will receive all depend on the individual policy you select. First, review what you already have. Your homeowner's or renter's policy probably covers your personal effects when you travel. You must evaluate your personal health and needs, destination (an adventure trip might require more insuring than a trip to Kansas), and costs.

- **Trip cancellation/trip interruption insurance** may be worth the price if you have prepaid for a tour or cruise. Trip insurance reimburses you for whatever part of your prepayment you can't recover from the tour or cruise operator. Most people plan a major trip as much as a year in advance and it is difficult to predict what might happen in that period of time. Think about anything that could force you to cancel or interrupt your trip. Do you have a medical condition that could flare up and cause a cancellation? How about a sick relative?

- **Emergency medical evacuation policies** pay the cost of transportation to a medical facility in the event of serious injury or illness that cannot be treated locally. Imagine breaking a leg while touring in China. You want to be cared for in a hospital with Western medicine and standards, but how can you get there? Some policies will arrange and pay for a helicopter or private jet to take you to the closest acceptable medical facility and then transportation home.

Policies are generally "bundled" or sold as a package containing both trip cancellation/interruption coverage and emergency medical evacuation. They may also include accident, baggage delay or loss, collision/damage waiver, medical/hospital, and trip delay.

Travel insurance availability is based on country of residence. To learn about travel insurance for your home country online, use the search term "travel insurance ___ resident" and insert your country of residence. The following companies offer policies to travelers who are United States residents:

Access America
800.284.8300
www.accessamerica.com

MEDEX
800.732.5309
www.medexassist.com

AIG/Travel Guard
800.826.4919
www.travelguard.com

Medjet Assist
800.5ASSIST (527.7478)
www.medjetassist.com

CSA
800.873.9855
www.csatravelprotection.com

Travel Insured International
800.243.3174
www.travelinsured.com

Health Care Abroad
800.237.6615
www.wallach.com

Travelex
800.228.9792
www.travelex-insurance.com

International SOS Assistance
800.523.8930
www.internationalsos.com

Worldwide Assistance
800.777.8710
www.worldwide/assistance.com

CHAPTER 27

The Last Word...
Going Home

Stay alert on the return trip — problems often occur
when you are tired and focused on going home.

All good trips must come to an end — and that means you must pack everything back into your bags and head home. And, if you're like most travelers, you'll have more stuff to pack than what you packed in your bags the day before you left — treasures, souvenirs, or business papers do take up space. In addition, experienced travelers will tell you there is no logic to this, but dirty clothes always seem to take up more room than clean clothes.

Packing for the Return Trip

The reality is that the car, train, or plane are still the same size as when you left and the rules about the number of bags haven't changed either. So, here are some ways to manage packing for your return:

- Repack your things with as much care as you took when you left home; that way, you'll stand a chance that everything will fit back into the bag.

- Pack your accumulated non-breakables into the empty nylon bag you packed (see page 105) and check it. Or, fill the bag with your dirty laundry and put your acquisitions in the suitcase. Check both.

- If your airline will allow another carry-on, pack your breakable or precious acquisitions into the nylon bag and take it on board. Wrap fragile items in bubble wrap or layers of clothing and place on top of a heavy sweater (as a cushion) in the bottom of the bag. Pack additional clothing around the piece. Place this under the seat in front of you to avoid someone crushing it with a heavy carry-on bag in the overhead bin.

- Ship things home. If you have been to a convention and have a ton of paper that you want but don't need tomorrow, get a box and some strapping tape, wrap it up, and send it home. Post offices and shipping companies worldwide will both quote rates over the phone if you know the destination zip code and approximate weight. This works for extra clothing, unbreakable souvenirs — anything that will lighten your load. And it works worldwide. Some hotels will wrap and ship for you for a fee.

SMART TRAVEL

Plan to send things home throughout the trip. Pack several large envelopes and send back maps and guidebooks you've used and paper you've added but don't want to lug around with you.

SHOPPER'S ALERT

Each time you use an item acquired on a trip, you will recall special memories. I buy coffee mugs and remember special places each day with my morning pick-me-up. My sister Nancy K. relives her trips each time she wears a garment made from her away-from-home fabric purchases. Barbara W. buys new ornaments for her Christmas tree.

If shopping is a primary pastime during your travels, plan ahead and take shopping and shipping supplies with you.

For shopping:
- Extremely comfortable shoes
- Shopping tote or backpack
- Gift list with recipients' sizes
- Color swatches of wardrobe and home colors
- Measurements of table (for buying tablecloths)
- Tape measure (avoid metal cases as they set off airport security)
- Large envelope for receipts (you will need these for Customs declarations on international trips; read "What About Customs?" on next page)

For shipping:
- Bubble wrap
- Scissors (blunt point required if put in carry-on)
- Strapping tape
- Sturdy, zip-top nylon bag

What About Customs?

When you return home from an international trip, you will pass through Customs. The agent's job is to ensure that people entering the country aren't bringing anything illegal or harmful with them. You will be asked to declare things you bought while traveling. If you are an American resident, before you leave the United States, read the booklet *Know Before You Go* from US Customs (see page 240) to learn what you can and cannot bring into this country and all about "Exemptions."

This is how customs works. During your return flight, you will be given a declaration form to fill out before you arrive at your first stop inside the destination country. For example, if you are landing in Los Angeles and changing planes for Phoenix, you will go through US Customs in LA. You may be asked to produce receipts for your purchases, and the Customs agent may want to see what you bought. They may also inspect *all* of your luggage.

Here's how to prepare for Customs during your trip and pass through Customs quickly.

1. **Be prepared.** Know what is and is not allowed so that you will not be tempted to bring back carved ivory from China or sausages from Germany. Prohibited articles will be confiscated and you lose.

2. **Be organized.** Save all your receipts in a large envelope. Convert your purchases from foreign currency to your local currency and write this amount on each receipt. I keep a running list of purchases in the envelope so I have less to fill out on the customs declaration. Keep this envelope with all your receipts in your most accessible carry-on. Pack all of your purchases at the top of one suitcase; if asked to produce purchases you won't have to spend an hour looking through four bags.

3. **Be honest.** Customs agents are very savvy people. Every possible trick that could be pulled has been unsuccessfully attempted by pros much better than you. The agents know your necklace is quality jade and that you paid more than the phony receipt shows. They know the difference between real luxury goods and knock-offs (which can be seized). Declare everything you have purchased; at most the duty might be 10% of the purchase price for items over your allowable exemption. Duty owed may be paid by check or credit card.

4. **Be smart.** Not a hint of drugs should have been close to you or your luggage. Every international baggage claim area has dogs trained to sniff out even a trace of drugs. David and I watched a man die a thousand deaths as a shrewd Customs agent ran a fingernail around the inside corners of his suitcase and found tiny shreds of marijuana a beagle had sniffed out.

5. **Be presentable.** Even if you have just completed a grueling trek in Nepal, make a huge effort to be clean and tidy. The more professional you look, the lower your odds of being questioned extensively or searched. Think about yourself standing unshaven, with an agent going through your luggage with a fine tooth comb. If you look suspicious, Customs has the right to grill you. The opposite is true, too. If you look like the queen of shopping and declare nothing, you'll be searched — guaranteed!

Time to Unpack

As you are unpacking, take a few minutes to reflect on your trip and make note of the following:

- How did your clothing work? Which pieces served you well and which were losers? This will help you pack for the next trip.

- What did you forget that you really needed? Put that item at the top of your packing list so you'll remember it the next time.

- What did you *not* have that would have been handy? Add this to the list too. File your notated list so you can edit it quickly when planning your next trip.

- How did your luggage perform? Any damage? Did you encounter someone on your travels who had the bag of your dreams? If so, start shopping now while it is fresh on your mind.

- Did you have all necessary toiletries, cosmetics, and health supplies? Update your list and restock your travel kit so they are ready to go when you take off for your next fabulous trip.

Even though you are tired of travel and so happy to be back home in your own bed, I know that you are already planning the next trip. Here's to smart packing and safe and enjoyable travel!

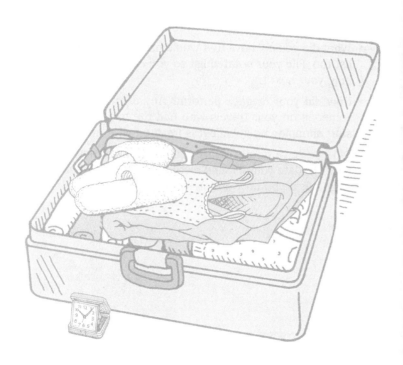

Resources

Travel Clothing
All offer online shopping
*also Travel Accessories and
Luggage

Banana Republic
Catalog and stores
888.BRSTYLE (277.8953)
www.bananarepublic.com

Bloomingdale's*
Catalog and stores
800.777.0000
www.bloomingdales.com

Chico's
Catalog and Stores
888.855.4986
www.chicos.com

Coldwater Creek
Catalog and stores
800.262.0040
www.coldwatercreek.com

Duluth Trading Co.*
Catalog
800.505.8888
www.duluthtrading.com

Eddie Bauer*
Catalog and stores
800.426.8020
www.eddiebauer.com

Ex Officio
Manufacturer with stores
800.644.7303
www.exofficio.com

J. Crew
Catalog and stores
800.562.0258
www.jcrew.com

J. Jill
Catalog and stores
800.642.9989
www.jjill.com

Lands' End*
Catalog
800.356.4444
www.landsend.com

L.L. Bean/L.L.Bean Traveler*
Catalog
800.221.4221
www.llbean.com

Macy's/Macy's By Mail*
Catalog and stores
800.BUY MACY (289.6229)
www.macys.com

Magellan's*
Catalog
800.962.4943
www.magellans.com

Neiman Marcus
Catalog and stores
800.825.8000
www.neimanmarcus.com

Nordstrom
Catalog and stores
800.285.5800
www.nordstrom.com

Norm Thompson*
Catalog
800.547.1160
www.NormThompson.com

Orvis
Catalog and stores
800.541.3541
www.orvis.com

Patagonia*
Catalog and stores
800.638.6464
www.patagonia.com

SAF-T-POCKETS™ Patterns
Travel Clothing and
Accessories
503.761.6460
www.saf-t-pockets.com

Sahalie* (formerly
Early Winters) Catalog
800.458.4438
www.sahalie.com

Saks Fifth Avenue
Catalog and stores
800.347.9177
www.saks.com

Sun Precautions
Catalog
800.882.7860
www.sunprecautions.com

The Territory Ahead
Catalog
800.882-4323
www.territoryahead.com

Tilley Endurables
Catalog
800.363.8737
www.tilley.com

Title Nine Sports
Catalog
800.609.0092
www.title9sports.com

TravelSmith*
Catalog
800.950.1600
www.travelsmith.com

Weekenders
Direct Sales
847-229-1200
www.weekenders.com

WinterSilks
Catalog
800.648.7455
www.wintersilks.com

Travel Accessories/Luggage

Brookstone
Catalog and stores
800.351.7222
www.brookstone.com

Christine Columbus
On-line retailer
800.280.4775
www.christinecolumbus.com

eBags
On-line retailer
800.820.6126
www.ebags.com

Lillian Vernon
Catalog
800.545.5426
www.lillianvernon.com

Minimus
On-line retailer
Travel-sized products
www.minimus.biz

REI
Catalog and stores
800.426.4840
www.rei.com

The Sharper Image
Catalog and stores
800.344.4444
www.sharperimage.com

Sky Roll® Luggage
Manufacturer
www.skyroll.com

Solutions
Catalog
800.342.9988
www.SolutionsCatalog.com

TUTTO® Luggage
800.949.1288
www.tutto.com

Publications

Conde Nast Traveler
800.777.0700
www.cntraveler.com

Consumer Reports
www.consumerreports.org

Cruise Diva
On-line Cruise Planner
www.CruiseDiva.com

National Geographic Traveler
800.NGS.LINE (647.5463)
www.ngtraveler.com

Travel & Leisure
800.888.8728
www.travelandleisure.com

Travel Smart
800.327.3633
www.travelsmartnewsletter.com

Organizations

American Society of Travel
Agents (ASTA)
www.asta.org
www.travelsense.org

American Society of Tropical
Medicine and Hygiene
847.480.9592
www.astmh.org

Association of Sewing and
Design Professionals
(formerly PACC)
877.755.0303
www.sewingprofessionals.org

Centers for Disease Control
and Prevention (CDC)
877. FYI TRIP (394.8747)
www.cdc.gov/travel

Federal Aviation
Administration (FAA)
866.TELL FAA (835.5322)
www.faa.gov

Federal Citizen
Information Center
(Order Government
Publications)
888.878.3256
www.pueblo.gsa.gov

International Association for
Medical Assistance to
Travelers (IAMAT)
716.754.4883
www.iamat.org

International Society of
Travel Medicine
707.736.7060
www.istm.org

Transportation Security
Administration (TSA)
866.289.9673
www.tsa.gov

Travel Goods Association (TGA)
609.720.1200
www.travel-goods.org

US Customs Service
Know Before You Go
(on-line booklet)
www.customs.gov

US Department of
Transportation
http://safetravel.dot.gov
Fly Rights (on-line booklet)
http://airconsumer.ost.dot.gov
/publications/flyrights.htm

US State Department Travel
Warnings, Travel Alerts
www.travel.state.gov

World Health Organization
(WHO)
www.who.org

Safety Information

Corporate Travel Safety
Detective Kevin Coffey
800.601.5711
www.corporatetravelsafety.com

Luggage Services

Luggage Concierge
800.288.9818
www.luggageconcierge.com

Luggage Express
(now part of Sports Express)
866.SHIP BAGS (744.7224)
www.usxpluggageexpress.com

Luggage Forward
866.416.7447
www.luggageforward.com

Luggage Free
800.361.6871
www.luggagefree.com

SkyCap International
877.775.9227
www.skycapinternational.com

Sports Express
800.357.4174
www.sportsexpress.com

Virtual Bellhop
(now part of Sports Express)
877.BELLHOP (235.5467)
www.virtualbellhop.com

Bibliography

Axtell, Roger E. *Do's and Taboos Around the World*, Third Edition (John Wiley & Sons, Inc., 1993).

Bezruchka, Dr. Stephen. *The Pocket Doctor: A Passport to Healthy Travel*, Third Edition (The Mountaineers, 1999).

Bond, Marybeth, editor. *A Woman's World: True Life Stories of World Travel*, (Travelers' Tales, 2007).

Bond, Marybeth. *Gutsy Women: More Travel Tips and Wisdom for the Road*, Third Edition (Travelers' Tales, 2007).

Chic Simple (Kim Johnson, Jeff Stone). *Dress Smart Men: Wardrobes That Win in the New Workplace* (Alfred A. Knopf, 2002).

Chic Simple (Kim Johnson Gross, Jeff Stone). *Men's Wardrobe* (Alfred A. Knopf, 1998).

Coffey, Detective Kevin. *Traveler Beware,* audio book CD (Corporate Travel Safety, 2007)

Kelly, Clinton, and Stacy London. *Dress Your Best: The Complete Guide to Finding the Style That's Right for Your Body*, (Three Rivers Press, 2005).

Mulari, Mary. *Made for Travel* (Krause Publications, 2002).

Nix-Rice, Nancy. *Looking Good* (Palmer/Pletsch Publishing, 1996).

Savage, Peter. *The Safe Travel Book,* Revised Edition (Lexington Books, 1999).

Whitman, Beth. *Wanderlust and Lipstick: The Essential Guide for Women Traveling Solo*, (Globe Trekker Press, 2007).

Zepatos, Thalia. *A Journey of One's Own*, Third Edition (Eighth Mountain Press, 2003).

Acknowledgements

I am forever grateful to my niece Peggy Hughes Frede who created the concept for this book by saying "Your travel tips are terrific, you should write a book." Twelve years later I finally did it.

Thanks to my frequent traveler friends listed below who so generously completed a survey that provided many interesting quotes, personal experiences and tips. Special thanks to Sheila Bates, Rosemary Barnhart, Kathleen Lenn, and Lisa McElhinny whose responses were so creative that they inspired me to expand the scope of the book.

Many thanks to my editor and dear friend Barbara Weiland, my special wordsmith Marilyn Morse, and to the endless creativity of Linda Wisner and Wisner Creative — all were wonderfully helpful.

Marta Alto
Ruth Arksey
Barbara Ash
Norma Barnhisel
Margie Bergstrom
Sid Blitz
Gail Brown
Roberta Carr
Mary Danielson
Nancy Di Cocco
Karen Dillon
Tim Filkins
Dorothy C. Foster
Bridget Gilmour
Linda Goldsmith
Len Goodman
Linda Griepentrog
Roxanne and Tom Heilpern
June Hughes
Liesje Hughes
Deni Jenkins
Jerry Jones
Nancy Kores
Ellen Kropp-Rogers

Peggy Lumpkin
Sonya McDowell
Marilyn Reed Merino
Lenada Merrick
Marcy Miller
Nancy S. Mueller
Nancy Nevin
Pati Palmer
Sharon Perry
Bill Pletsch
Bob Powers
Lynn Raasch-Benson
Liz and Andy Rapp
JoAnn Rosen
Marion Sato
Jackie Shearer
Roz Simon
June Smith
Barbara Stewart
Judy Sumka
Terri and Grant Todd
Sue Tysko
Leslie and Jeffrey Willmott

INDEX

To order additional copies of *Smart Packing for Today's Traveler* at $19.95 plus $4.75 shipping and handling, send check or money order in US funds only to:

Smart Travel Press
P.O. Box 25514
Portland, OR 97298-0514

Or visit the website at www.smartpacking.com

The type was set in 9.5 Adobe Leawood Medium with Kabel Black heads and subheads, Lucida Sans captions.

The book was printed by Bang Printing, Brainerd, MN (coordinated by BookPrinters Network, Portland, OR), in a direct-to-plate process on 60# Husky Recycled Offset paper, 20% recycled.